# THE
# LOST ART OF
# **DISCIPLINE**

## THE PREREQUISITE FOR VICTORY

## CHAD HOWSE

*To my folks.*

# PREFACE

I, possibly like yourself, have always struggled with discipline. In those periods where I'm disciplined I'm free from financial stress, there is no worry about what must be done because it gets done. I'm in shape, I have more time, more power, less guilt about not being good enough. Then, however, I allow it to leave.

In the times where I lack discipline my life is aimless. I go from winner to wanderer and my goals give way to desires in the moment that take me further from the life I want to build, and the man I want to become.

I *know* it's value. In every book I've read about a great man who's accomplished incredible, daring feats, discipline was at the core, the foundation of what he was able to achieve. It is the path to victory in life, no matter how you define it. But knowing that something is good for you and making it not just a part of your life, but *who you are*, is another thing altogether.

Most people know what's best for them but few act on it every day, and the few that do live purposeful, successful lives.

This book breaks the barrier between intention and action. Discipline isn't just for some and not for others. You are not a naturally disciplined person, or someone who innately lacks discipline. You are what you've done thus far, how you've acted, the habits you've developed, but they can be changed, and in this book I'll show you how to do so.

Which is also why *I needed this book*. I saw how being disciplined can get me what I want in life, and how a lack of it can do the opposite, bring failure and aimlessness. I needed to *become disciplined*, to figure out how to do what I set out to do and not let anything stand in the way of what I want *most* in life and who I want to become.

In these pages I've drawn battle lines, brought clarity, asked good questions, all in an effort to remove excuses and bring forth victory in the moment, in the day, and in life.

I've applied everything in this book, and it's altered how I act, the work I do, the pride I have in who I am becoming, and I cannot wait for you to do the same.

If you want to accomplish something, anything, if you want to improve, to get better, to **by the end of your days be able to *know* that you used your time here in impressive fashion,** then discipline is something you *must* develop.

Many of us also hold back on developing discipline because we think that what we truly and audaciously want in life isn't for us. We think that our lofty goals are things that only 'the others' achieve. Well, again, we're all wrong about this. In the coming pages I give you examples from history, from periods and times when your birthplace and station in life really did determine your future, and yet, men who were born poor, into slavery, or into nations that were recently conquered, rose to wealth, power, and to positions that changed the trajectory of the planet.

What's most powerful is that I could have used *many* more examples from varying walks of life as proof that, no matter where you're born, the parents you're born to, or even who you've been up to this point and what you've accomplished, you can change, evolve, and grow into the man that deep down you want to become, the man that's worthy of the grand vision you have for your life.

No matter who you are, where you are, or how you currently live, it is not too late.

# The Most Valuable Virtue on the Planet

*Winners embrace hard work. They love the discipline of it, the trade-off they're making to win. Losers, on the other hand, see it as punishment. And that's the difference.*

—*Lou Holtz*

No matter what you value in life, discipline is the virtue that will help you get it. Discipline isn't dependent on height or good looks. It doesn't care how naturally fast you are, how talented you may be, or how high you can jump. It's the most valuable virtue on the planet, and every human has equal ability to develop it.

**Discipline is the equalizer. It can turn a poor man into a wealthy man if he develops it, or turn a wealthy man into a poor man if he ignores it.**

It's development within your own life is necessary to achieve anything and everything you could possibly set your sights on. Yet most people either don't want it or think they're doomed and predisposed not to have it. This book will accomplish a few things for both sorts of people:

1. You'll get a deeper understanding of the importance of discipline in new ways and different areas of your life, and an idea of why—if you have any ambition at all—discipline must be at the core of who you are, how you live, and how you think.

2. You'll see discipline in a new light. It is not mere routine, but power. It isn't constriction, but freedom. Discipline, worked into every facet of life—from how we think to how we set goals to how we act daily and, indeed, to the very nature of our actions—will deliver what we want and beyond. Few people, however, look at discipline in the right light. Change how you see discipline, and you open yourself up to greater control over your life and where you intend to take it.

3. You'll discover how to be disciplined daily to ensure that you become who you most audaciously would like to become. You'll also learn how discipline is dying in modern daily life, while at the same time becoming *even more* crucial in today's society, where our minds are rarely quiet, where our attention is seldom focused, where discipline is a lost art.

**Discipline is a lost art.**

Never before in history have the influences to pull us away from the disciplined, successful, purposeful life been so abundant and integrated into our society.

We've begun to praise the desire in the moment as being an expression of who we are, and thus good. We give power to emotions even if they take us away from what we want to accomplish, who we want to become, and the life we'd ideally like to live. We're never bored. Our attention is always given to something, the phone, the app, the images we scroll, watching someone else live while we wish we could do the same.

It isn't just that we have the internet, and even while I'm writing these words I *could*, feasibly check my phone or a website and take myself out of the work that must be done without anyone knowing but myself. Or that rather than being born into a profession like we once were, like farming, the endless career options that now exist leave many lost, confused, and in disarray about what they should do and 'who they should become'. It's that our values, too, have shifted.

If we don't allow for a child to be proclaimed the victor, and instead reward mere participation, we don't praise values like hard work and discipline that create victory. We're training mediocrity, when no one wants it, but it's becoming acceptable.

We've begun to deem those who do great things as somehow innately exceptional - something I'll repeatedly disprove in this book - rather than digging deeper to see their habits and how they've used discipline and momentum to do things that most people cannot.

Discipline is a lost art because distractions are everywhere, but also because it's no longer revered as it should be. It's seen as confining, not liberating.

In this book you will learn how to develop discipline, gaining the freedom that comes with it. If you, however, *like* the excuses that are now common and valid in today's society, if you're okay with mediocrity, with living as someone who doesn't resemble who you can potentially be, then maybe this isn't the right book for you.

By its end you will have no excuses, there will be no valid

reasons as to why you're not living a more successful, powerful, prosperous life.

So, think about that. Do you *really* want victory? Do you *really* want success and power, meaning and accomplishment? If you do, you'll adopt the structures, tactics and habits in this book while completely turning your back on the lie that it's okay to have anything less.

In the same way that most won't work hard enough to *earn* the life they want, most won't develop the necessary discipline that this existence demands of them. They will remain as they are, living a life worthy only of mediocrity. But you will. You're different. While you're fighting an uphill battle, especially in this society, the mere fact that you're willing to admit that discipline is the path to who you want to become and the life you want to create sets you apart from a society content with watching from afar, commenting and gossiping and envying those brave souls who enter the arena and turn their backs on mediocrity.

While the societal trends may be moving toward a less disciplined, effective, happy and productive life, they're the trends of the masses and in no way have to align with your life and your story.

When we look at the collective, and how our days are lived and our minutes and seconds used and spent, we *are* more distracted than ever. A recent study in the *Harvard Business Review* found that people spend 47 percent of their time thinking about something other than what they're doing. That's not actually living, it's dreaming, existing in a reality that isn't actually real. How horrible is that?

Humans have never spent less time in the moment. When your attention is constantly wishing on the future and dwelling on the past, you will not experience the good that is in the present, nor will you accomplish that which you hope to achieve. The present moment was all there once was, no computers or cell phones to take us out of our life and into dreamland. The social media, the images people display to portray only who they want you to see them as, pulls many into a spectatorship, and away from living life well.

It's near impossible to appreciate where we are when we're comparing it to the selective imagery posted on a social media account. It's downright unlikely that you're going to stay in your lane, focus on your work and *your* dreams if your attention is spent watching someone else live theirs.

When we're talking about not being in the moment from an achievement standpoint, not a single thing that you want deep down in your heart of hearts can be earned with divided attention. You will not raise your family to the best of your ability with divided attention. You will not develop the skills you want to develop with divided attention. You will not earn as much money as you could if your work is done with divided attention. You will not be as happy or as successful if the ability to focus isn't something you possess and apply.

Discipline is a lost art amid so many opportunities to live undisciplined lives. There's good in this. When it's never been more difficult to be disciplined, and when more and more people live with a sense of entitlement rather than toughness, being disciplined and tough automatically puts you in a class of your own, above all of those waiting for a gift or a hand out or a blessing.

To wait for a blessing or a gift is idiotic. The gift is your intelligence, it's your ambition, it's your potential. The duty is to fulfill it through work, discipline, and persistence. My man, the gift has already been given. The blessing has already been handed to you. Use it.

Achieving your goals isn't dependent on luck or talent. Their achievement depends on who you are, and who you are is how you live everyday. To do the right things on the grandest scale is discipline, without which you will not live a purposeful, happy, meaningful life.

Who am I to talk about discipline, let alone teach it?

To be honest, this is a section of the book that my editor demanded I include, but something I've struggled writing. I am not so arrogant as to assume I'm an authority on discipline, which is a marketing rule you shouldn't admit - who wants to hear from someone who isn't an authority?

I'm not sure there *are* authorities on such topics, there are merely people who've grown to understand it, adopt it, include it into their lives, and those who study it and so forth.

I am not a teacher in the modern sense. I'm not someone who doesn't have skin in the game as Nassim Taleb puts it. My success or failure in life depends on discipline. I need to develop it or I fail, just like you need to develop it or you fail.

There is no helping hand coming, no lottery ticket to be cashed in, no genie waiting to grant a wish. What we want in life is dependent on who we are, and if we want to be great, good, effective, efficient, and successful people, we need discipline.

Discipline is a topic that's avoided. It's a topic that hasn't truly been delved into enough - though I'm not sure there is an 'enough' when it comes to this topic. It's something I need more of in my life, something I've learned to *have more of* in my life, and something every single human on the planet with an ounce of ambition needs if they're to live a life to be proud of, a life that benefits them, their family, and the rest of society.

Being such a necessity in my own life I've worked hard at ways to develop it better, and I've worked at it for a long time.

Discipline as brought me from being the snooze-button-pushing, sleeping-in, diet-ditching, broke, indebted guy that I'll show you how *not to be* in this book, to a guy that is moving toward a goal, a destination in a much more efficient fashion.

Take books, for example. Forget about business, growth, earnings and all that stuff. Let's focus on the work. For about a decade I've wanted to write a book. I've actually written 3 or 4 that were well over 200 pages that never saw the light of day. In each circumstance I lacked the discipline to see the projects through to fruition. Within the past 6 months, however, I've written two books. One is published and being sold at themandietbook.com, and this is the second.

Work is being done. Projects are being finished. I have a clarity and focus in my life that I've lacked for my *entire life*, and I owe it to the exploration that has occurred in writing this book, but also a couple periods in my life that taught me a lot about discipline, periods that provided a few lessons we'll cover in this book, along with many more lessons from historical figures who actually lived lives worth writing about - some of whom you've likely never heard of before.

Now, as my editor has pushed and pushed me to do, I'll have to talk about myself and my own journey for a moment. I understand the value in this. I'm what you'd call a 'normal fella', historical figures are difficult to see as normal because of the scope of what they've accomplished, as are some of the larger-than-life figures who write books and seem to be born with an innate greatness that appears to be impossible to replicate (it isn't, I'll show you how in this book).

I share your struggles, your roadblocks and barriers. Yet, I've figured - and am constantly figuring - this discipline thing out. In this book I've simplified it because that's what such things need. They need simplification because they're not actually that difficult. They need simplification because we need to get out of our own way more than we need anything else to come into our lives and save us.

If the tactics, ideas, and philosophies found in these pages can help *me* go from the guy I was to the guy I am, then they will help you do the same.

And let's be frank, I'm not where I eventually want to be, nor am I living as the man I eventually want to become. This process of improvement is lifelong, but my goodness, far too many of us are further behind than we should be. Had we adopted the ruthless, freeing discipline you'll read about in this book, we'd already be living our ideal life and living as the men we want to become. To add to that, if we don't develop this discipline now, we'll *end our lives with regret* grasping our souls like a python to its prey. This is something to fear, regret. This is something that should wake us up and force us to act in a better fashion now, rather than pushing this necessary evolution into the future, a future that we all know is uncertain and not guaranteed.

There were two specific periods in my life when I found myself lost, stuck in a rut, and failing. One was after I dropped out of college.

Basketball was why I was *at college*. I had no idea what I wanted to be in life, how I wanted to earn a living, or what career I wanted to pursue, but I knew that I wanted to play basketball.

I worked my ass off all throughout high school in an effort to get a scholarship to an American school. No full scholarship was offered, so I went to a local college in hopes of then advancing to a better school after a good initial season. I worked hard at basketball. Every morning I'd wake up and train before class and finish after practice to shoot. Over the years I developed some knee issues that wouldn't go away unless I left the sport, so I did.

Now, however, I really didn't have a reason to go to school. I'd continue to take classes for a time but eventually dropped out and entered the workforce where at least I'd be *paid* for my efforts.

The first job I got after I quit school was that of a salesman for a cell phone company. What a wonderful teacher a sales job is, and what a great and necessary skill selling is for any human in any walk of life. I actually did well initially, too. It was a new challenge, so I had discipline initially that helped me succeed, but discipline doesn't do much if it's brief, and as I worked my butt off but collected relatively small paychecks, the discipline began to wear off and I regressed in that line of work.

Without a real reason to train, a sport, something that measured conditioning daily, I started to get fat. I stopped going to the gym. I started spending more money than I was making. My first period not being an athlete saw my discipline decline, and eventually disappear.

I was wandering. Men are not bred to wander. We need a direction to head toward, a mission to carry out, an animal to hunt, a family to provide for, a goal to pursue. We need direction. I had it, but I didn't identify it, specifically, nor did I set out everyday to move toward it.

Life will inevitably see us hit down periods. We all experience them. They're a reality because life is tough and no matter how well you plan, life will do its best to derail said plans. Thus, since they're a constant, your skids or slides or ebbs are not just yours, but a constant amongst all men. You are not alone in your *feelings* to want to do nothing, to avoid work and be lazy. You're not special in that you *feel* like things aren't going your way. If anything in the human experience is shared, it's the struggle and its many forms. This, however, doesn't remove or change the fact that you're here for a reason and effort and pain and struggling are necessary for you to make that a good reason.

With that, it's on you to do whatever you can to get out of them. You do not wait to rise from the depths, to get out of a funk, you *get out of the funk*. Sometimes these 'downfalls' can happen over years, but the movement out of them can begin within minutes or seconds, with the simplicity and finality of a decision, a choice to move.

Again, you do not stay in the funk, you do *whatever* you can to climb out of it, however drastic or simple that upward trajectory may be.

Pain, practice, and training had been a part of my life for almost my entire life, and as that physicality left with basketball leaving, I began to live a more sedated life.

While an issue may be mental - or we see it as mental - there's power in having your body lead your recovery. If you look at our evolution as humans, we've *unevolved physically*. We're fatter, weaker, and unhealthier than we were centuries ago. We are not supposed to be fat. For men, it makes us carry too much estrogen, diminishing our most powerful and important hormone, testosterone, in the process. As our testosterone levels decline, we're more likely to experience depression.

As I became more sedentary having quit basketball, boxing jolted me back to the way of life I wanted to live. Pain led me back to the way of life I wanted to live.

Every man should take up some form of martial art in his lifetime. It's something we're lacking in our society where men don't feel like men because, well, many of us don't act like men because we *don't know how to act like men*, or we're too lazy to act like men. The confidence gained in the ring or the octagon or on the wrestling mat is immeasurable, and the lessons we learn about ourselves, invaluable.

Boxing has so much more nuance to it than the average spectator sees. It truly is a science. If you're good enough, you lead your opponent to do what you want him to do without him knowing that you're leading him anywhere. Then, as the rounds wear on it becomes a battle of attrition, where the man with the bigger heart, the stronger spirit, and the better preparation begins to dominate the mentally weaker opponent.

Boxing taught me about the discipline of habit and routine, the discipline of accepting pain in ever-greater amounts, and to be able to think in a disciplined manner, to not allow thoughts that did not help me into my brain, or at least to take up too much space. I learned that I could decide what to think about and that I had the power to react to an event in any way I wanted.

The discipline I learned from boxing gave me back power and control over my life right when I was losing it. This newfound outlook on discipline proved invaluable in my next stage of life: starting a business.

To make a very uninteresting story shorter and a tad more interesting, a friend of mine introduced me to the online world of writing programs for people and selling them. The world is your market, not your area code. You schedule emails and can make money while you're sleeping. You are your own boss, so you can work as little or as much as you want.

After selling phones for a relatively small commission lost its luster, and after growing frustrated and tired of personal training and the myriad of excuses my clients would have for not showing up or doing the work or sticking to their diet, working in solitude and working to build something sounded incredible.

If you've ever worked alone, you'll know that the discipline that comes from a boss is non-existent. You do the work or your don't. No one will reprimand you for not doing the work, you're just not going to make any money, grow your business, or make any ounce of an impact. If you work alone you have to create structures that make getting the work done the only option. The work you do doesn't depend on how you feel or what you feel like doing. It's a great teacher, and any author, entrepreneur, or self-employed human will know the necessity of self-control and proper habits when you're going at it alone.

What was more incredible were the success stories I came across early on. As I learned more about the entrepreneurial world I heard of guys starting businesses and making it into the 6 figure range within a matter of months; in fact, I'd seen guys very quickly get deep into seven figures in annual net revenue, so I expected to do the same. **But life rarely gives you what you want. It will give you only what you earn, and that ain't giving, that's taking, and I hadn't taken initial success.**

Initially, kept the personal training business going to fund the online business. That actually went on for a couple years until I realized that I was comfortable. The online gig didn't technically *need to work*, no matter how bad I wanted it to work, because of that second income source. I'm not sure if it's 'smart' to quit your only way of making money, as the online business was far from even being able to keep the lights on at this point, but I gave away the training business and focused only on trying to figure out how to create programs, courses, and books that people would not only benefit from, but that they'd actually buy online.

After a few months, I ran out of money and began acquiring debt fast. I had a period of eight months where I couldn't pay rent on time, but somehow, always a few days late, I'd have a check in hand for the landlord. That was stressful. There were times where I felt like the weight of the world was caving in on me. Maybe it was youthful ignorance, but I just figured that everything would work out so I kept working, paying rent late, and eating the cheapest, shittiest food I could get my hands on.

**Stress can bust pipes or make diamonds, and we get to *choose* which way it affects us and our lives.** Few are aware of this choice. We see stress as something happening to us, something we have no part in creating, but it's completely mental. And let's not gloss over the fact that there's *good stress*. We need stress to improve. We put our muscles under stress so that they grow, and we do the same when we want to build a business or improve at something. Life is a constant game of having your reach exceed your grasp. If we're trying to improve we're never truly comfortable, nor should we want to be.

There's also, of course, bad stress. It's the worry kind. It's our minds worrying about an outcome or an event that has yet to happen, and our minds can come up with evil, horrific, and scary outcomes that are really not likely at all.

We need the stress of having our reach exceed our grasp, but we do not need the stress that comes from self-imposed worrying.

Years later my old man had an interesting outlook on why so

many men are depressed and killing themselves today. It's merely one cause of many, but it's interesting nonetheless and it helps explain an outlook that helped me get through this period.

I asked my dad the question, *why are men more depressed now even though life is easier and our quality of life is better?*

His answer focused on my grandfather's generation, the Greatest Generation. The generation that grew up amidst the Great Depression, went to fight in the Second World War, and then came home and went to work without complaint, without talking about their feelings or feeling as though life isn't fair. My old man said, **Men used to expect life to be difficult, today we expect it to be easy and when it proves to be difficult, we break.**

My old man's dad worked three jobs to support his family. My other grandfather fought for Italy in the Second World War in Siberia, where he had to take the life of his best friend who got extreme frostbite. His best friend. Let that sink in. There were other things he had to do, horrors that he only later confessed on his deathbed to my dad, a man he thought was a priest (he isn't, though there's no one I'll ever meet that's closer to the Man Upstairs). He carried them with him for life, up until days before his death, and yet never saw them as unfair or reasons to quit. After the war he moved his family of 8 to Canada where he worked in a precious metals plant for most of the remainder of his life where he lost at least one finger (I can't remember if there was more than one finger lost, but one was gone for sure). If you've ever seen one of those factories you'll know that it's hard work.

Then he got cancer, either from smoking or just as likely from where he worked, and he died.

His wife is a tough broad. My Nonna fought off Germans who invaded her house during the latter stages of the Second World War, a story I'll tell in more detail later. My mom's tough. My dad's tough. That generation coined as the Greatest Generation, though, did what was expected of them, and the expectations they had weighing on their shoulders are far greater than those of our coddled, modern youth (my generation included).

It was likely because of the struggle they grew up in, the Great Depression. It is true that tough times develop tough men and those tough men then create good times which, in turn, produce weak men who then - through their softness - create tough times once again and the cycle repeats itself.

Toughness, however, doesn't need poverty to be developed, it simply requires discipline, often the discipline to bring pain into one's life rather than aiming to avoid it.

My dad's outlook on the modern depression crisis amongst middle class men - at least in my mind - is profound. How we view the world shapes how we react to life's inevitable tribulations. The tribulation is always there, it will always come. The fact is that life *is hard*, and with bigger goals and greater aspirations, you're making your life necessarily more arduous. You cannot avoid the tribulation and win, so ignoring it, wishing it would not exist, and being blind to its existence will see you live a life of failure, of laziness, and with depression as your constant companion.

The acceptance of tribulation is a must. On the inner part of my left arm I have a wonderful verse that reminds me of that fact. *You will have tribulation, take courage, I have overcome the world.* You **will** have tribulation. It's a part of this human experience. To pout about it - as we all do from time to time - really doesn't do you any good, in fact, it usually distorts reality, making a tough situation seem hopeless, though they never are.

All you can do is to do all you can do. If you work persistently you're making a positive outcome very likely. If you're a worker, if you have discipline, an outlook that 'everything will workout' is a logical one. If you're lazy but you're still an optimist, you're just lying to yourself and that ignorance will bite you in the future.

Life never gets easier, and ease isn't necessarily something you should want. Compare how you feel when you sleep in and then watch TV all day (hopefully this never happens), to how you feel when you get up at the crack of dawn to go workout or work or run. They're incomparable. That doesn't make getting up at 4am easier. It's never easy. It is, however, better, and that's not something you can even argue if you've done either for an extended period of time. Discipline's reward is both the achievement in the end and the present satisfaction that comes from living well.

There's something in all of us that understands that quitting is for losers and that being disciplined is how we live if we want to win. We feel horrible if we sleep in and waste a day, yet it's repeatedly done because our lives lack the framework to create disciplined habits. So, we expect to one day develop it magically, ignoring how life works.

I stuck with the online business in part because my folks never made me think that life was easy, nor that I deserved what I did not have. If they had, I would have quit early and this book would have never been written. They congratulated me on work well done when I was growing up, and praised hard work as a virtue. They did not fight my battles for me. That desire to get your kid better grades and doing their project for them rips them of both the effort *they* needed to put into the project, and the possibility of negative feedback and ridicule from other classmates that would inevitably come if they did shitty work or no work at all.

With all of that said, this was the first time I'd really stuck with *anything*. I don't think it needed to be this. I could have done well had I stuck with a construction job I had, or a sales job, or anything, really. I mentioned this relationship with money, and not wanting to be paid per hour, but that can be bullshit. If you have a construction job you're not *just* being paid by the hour, you're learning. You're watching the boss, seeing how things can be improved, providing value to your employer, saving, and someday starting your own business.

At the time I didn't want a boss. I was a stubborn kid who

wanted to work hard while not being confined by the set rules of a company or organization. However, the key word is that I was *a kid*, mentally at least. There were opportunities to rise and grow in every job I had, I was often just too ignorant and closed-minded to see them.

When I *did* finally grow up mentally and see that jumping from job-to-job, career-to-career, had me starting from the bottom every time I quit, how my folks raised me and what they taught me about hard work and making your own way in life really did help. I used to hate that I had to pay for my own jockey equipment as a kid, or that I had a paper route before I was legally allowed to work or have one, or that I had to work full-time every summer, again, before I was legally allowed to work, even working as a mechanic's assistant at a family friend's garage. But holy hell is learning the value of a dollar, and the gift that is work - any work - more valuable than playing with your friends day in and day out every summer.

Now, I was still boxing, getting up early to run and showing up to the gym at 5pm daily, and decided to treat my new business like I treated boxing rather than treating it like a hobby or a passion project like I was initially. In training for boxing there are things you just do, and things you don't do. It's simple. You run, lift, and spar. You eat healthy. You hydrate. And you repeat these habits daily. In my work, I created habits that I just did without thought. I wrote religiously every morning, tallying over 5,000 words a day on articles and courses.

I *needed* this structure because I needed to do more work because I realized that I needed more *failure* to find success than the fellas I knew who were growing their businesses and their following much more quickly than I was. I needed to produce more programs and content so I could see what *didn't work* and thus eventually find out what *did*. I wasn't as innately good - nor am I now - as others, so I have to do a little more work to see what will succeed, what will fail, and then double down on what succeeds. It's something I'm realizing more often these days, that I might have to do a little more work than the average fella to create the success I want. It may have to do with the goals I have, or with how I learn, or with how savvy I am or am not business-wise.

Initially the work was being done but the success wasn't coming. I created a bunch of products, and one by one they failed. Now, 'success' back then would have been making enough money to pay my damn bills. That was the initial goal. Yet, with each venture I saw failure. I was learning *what not to do* so I could learn what *to do*, and what *to do* eventually came when I decided to focus on fixing my own problems, doing the research to solve my own issues, then taking what works and creating books and programs and courses out of what has proven to work for me and others.

How simple.

The first victory was *The Man Diet*, now a book that you can get for free at theManDietbook.com. I had less than optimal testosterone levels. This can lead to a host of issues like low drive, increased body fat, low energy, and even depression. I studied how to solve said issue for a few years, and then put everything that worked and what was holding my testosterone levels back, into book form.

That single idea, a program that helps guys naturally increase their testosterone levels (low testosterone is becoming somewhat epidemic, with men's testosterone levels declining by 1.2%-1.3% annually, regardless of age according to a study out of the University of Massachusetts) eventually enabled me to do *more* than just pay my bills, helping me travel the world for a year, earning all the while, so that I had a heck of a lot more money when I returned than when I left. It helped me grow my following and the impact of my business and, more, it proved to me that being broke wasn't who I was but rather the result of what I'd been doing.

This book is no different. I struggled with discipline. I knew

I needed to develop it, to figure out some tactics and strategies to gain it if I was going to live any semblance of a good life. So, study and test, I did, and everything that has worked is in this book.

Before, however, I even *thought* about this book, those decisions to walk into a boxing gym and fight for a few years and then to start my own business forced me to become a student of discipline. It was either create the right habits and find some success, or keep living as a victim to desires in the moment and exist forever as a dependent, a victim, a failure. The thing is, I don't think I'm alone in having to make that decision. Which is why I figured this book was more than just a pet project, but a damn necessity for a lot of men like myself.

**We need discipline. Society is hell-bent on having us not develop it.**

Trying to improve at both boxing and business helped me develop self-discipline. While I think boxing and business are two of the best teachers a fella can have, aiming to improve at anything, be it writing, hunting, shooting, or parenting, will require the development of discipline. Boxing, especially, forced upon me the appreciation of inconvenience. That is, especially in boxing, I had to do things that I didn't want to do, and not only did I have to do them, I grew to understand their necessity, and even aim to make them *more* inconvenient. It's the things that are the most inconvenient in boxing, the long runs in the morning or at night, that help you develop the toughness you need in the latter rounds of a fight.

When long runs become routine, you have to do them earlier. When it's raining or snowing outside, the run still has to happen and it has to occur when you *least* want to do it. To do it when it's most convenient is easy. Everyone can do easy. Easy doesn't help you improve like inconvenience does, like difficulty does, like pain does.

When you live a life of active and purposeful inconvenience

you put yourself into a very exclusive class of human where the competition isn't that stiff. The competition isn't among the greats, it's among the masses, where mediocre humans - billions of them - do mediocre work, put forth mediocre effort, and all compete to get mediocre results, jobs, and salaries.

The elite - and I do not mean *the elites*, but the high-performers, the grittier, tougher, more stoic and even more brutal humans among us - have fewer people to compete against. Moreover, they stay in their lane, not concerned about the periphery or what someone else is doing, they're too busy working, earning, evolving, to care about how another human is living. Additionally, they're rarely competition *against* one another, rather, they're competing alongside one another, often in different fields, or if they're in the same industry, their growth isn't deterred by the growth of another.

When you start adopting a more inconvenient lifestyle, one where you take the hard path - and the smart path - and do the work that must be done not only to win, but to acquire the grit that victory requires, you begin to separate yourself from the rest of humanity.

Not that I separated myself from the rest of humanity, but by trying to become a better boxer, and seeing the necessity of both toughness and conditioning in such a quest, adopting a lifestyle that sought difficulty and pain was incredibly invaluable, and will remain valuable until I kick the bucket.

Theodore Roosevelt speaks a wonderful truth in the following quote:

> *"Nothing in this world is worth having or worth doing unless it means effort, pain, difficulty."*

We've become a society focused on ease and convenience

when both bring us further away from what we want and who we want to become to get what we want.

Not only do we have to pursue more difficult things in our lives so as to develop the toughness that comes from doing such things, but we have to do it alone. Self-discipline is discipline. It is of no value to you to have discipline that comes only from oversight. That is, someone telling you to do something. That doesn't count. You need to walk this road alone, that's where power and strength come from, from solitude, from your spirit and soul and not from an outside force forcing it upon you.

The thing about boxing is that you can *tell* who's doing their roadwork in the morning by what happens in the gym later that evening. I had no overseer watching my morning runs when I was fighting or my morning work block when I started my business, and the failure to develop self-discipline in either boxing or business would see me getting my ass kicked in the former, and broke and, well, broken in the latter. I wanted to avoid failure almost as much as I wanted to succeed, and by choosing two 'professions' where failure was drastic and crushing, but also largely solo ventures, the success of both rested on my daily persistent and consistent actions and not on a structure defined and implemented by a company or a boss.

As you'll read in the coming pages and chapters, discipline is often just a matter of doing what you set out to do, and while it takes discipline to think about what the right thing to do is, carrying out that task or action requires little, if any, thought. It's a removal of options, and many of the options we have in life are creations of the mind in an effort to avoid the work that must get done. In short, options are often excuses, nothing more.

As you learn to shut off the voice that rationalizes doing something other than what you've set out to do, you make discipline automatic. This automation doesn't make you robotic, it makes you effective. It turns you from a dreamer or a dabbler to a doer. It turns your intentions into actions and accomplishments. Removing the voices and opinions in your own mind that constantly want you to do what's easiest rather than what's best enables you to live, and live well. You create this lack of thought when it comes to acting by setting fewer, better tasks, and acting upon them habitually.

You do not become less creative, rather, you're more creative because you're giving time to creativity. When it comes to action, creativity is no longer needed, it's time to act and that doesn't require analysis.

As I made a morning run routine, as I did it 10 days in a row, then 20, then 30, it became less of a grand quest and more of a habit. It was always tough, that's the point of running at 5 in the morning, but whether or not it was done wasn't a consideration.

To be transparent here, this habit wasn't created easily. Actually, yes it was, what am I saying. Eventually I just decided to make it a habit and it became a habit. But my naturally lazy ass resisted forming this habit for a long time. I stood in my own way. Sound familiar? This discipline thing is less complicated than we want it to be. We want it to be complicated because complicated things are better solved for another day or by another person. Discipline, the act of doing things that will get you what you want most in life, is simple. You decide what's the best thing for you to do, and you do it.

The same happened with my morning writing block - you'll hear more about this tactic later in the book. At first, I would focus on writing for only 20 minutes at a time, then I pushed it to 40, then 60, and so on. Sitting down to write eventually became something that wasn't spectacular like I thought it was initially, it became habitual, something that was done seven days a week, like waking up and brushing my teeth.

We all know that discipline is valuable, but we don't quite

understand *how* valuable. Throughout our lives we're told that talent or birthright or blessings are what create high achievement. We're told about the muse, about ideas coming from nowhere that result in transformative companies or experiences or inventions. They're lies. When you realize that it is discipline that will get you what you want, you gain control of your present, which allows anyone the power to guide their life to an ideal future.

For a decade now, I've been getting emails every day from guys who are struggling with training, diets, work, relationships, money, and decisions about what they want, including who they want to be. Without exception, the solution can be broken down to an area of their lives that, if they had more discipline, would guarantee that they'd be thriving rather than struggling.

**This book will not provide you with someone to blame.**

Some humans like having someone or something to blame for where they are in life because it gives them a valid reason to not 'give it their all'. When you have a reason for being a failure that's outside of your actions, you have a reason to not do what success demands you do. This belief that anything or anyone but ourselves are responsible for our present and our future is just a belief, it's a perspective. If you want to be envious, bitter, and resentful, and if you want to accomplish nothing while pitying where you are and your place in life, then it's the correct perspective. It will give you what you want.

If, however, you want accomplishment, achievement, and the pride and power that comes from taking ownership and responsibility of every aspect of your life, then it's the wrong perspective. If you want to win, take responsibility for your life and every aspect of your life. If you want to be lazy, then blame people for your life.

The reality is that we are exactly where we deserve to be. This book will take this *belief* and turn it into reality. That is, we're going to look at different ways our culture and our society make it acceptable, even logical, to blame others, and we're going to disprove such things as myth. By the time you've read half of this book, you'll understand that you have *real power*, and that you control your future by taking ownership of both it, your past, and your present.

This book will destroy any merit you may think you have in blaming others, and that's incredibly good, because you do not want to give someone else power over your life, that's something that should rest in your hands and be seen in your thoughts and actions.

Here I must confess that I've written this book as much for me as for you. I've developed discipline over the past few years. I've seen how it can help a man go from a wisher to a winner, a dabler to a doer. I've experienced the peace that living a disciplined life brings to a man, the power it gives him over his future, and the pride it can give a man in who he is, what he's doing, and where he's going.

I've also experienced the *destructive* power of discipline's absence. I've felt the weight of debt. I've felt the pain of being a wanderer, of lacking direction, of feeling as though there's no real reason for my existence, **ignoring the fact that I can *decide* what my reason for being here is.** I've felt both powerful and power-less, and I don't ever want to feel powerless again. I want more discipline in my life. I want to understand why I make certain excuses and how I disguise them as 'reasons', or how I reason with myself to avoid doing what must be done when there is really only one option in front of me.

I *really* want to build something, to create a legacy, to make an impact, and I've seen the evidence of how impossible it is to doing such things without being extremely disciplined.

This book has been such a beneficial exercise for myself, that I know it will yield the same benefit to the reader, you. I wrote this to better understand discipline, to understand how to make it the only option, to know how to find clarity and remove the desires in the moment that take me away from my overall desire for my life.

I'm writing these few paragraphs after having finished the book. I started writing it having discovered a good deal about how to become more disciplined. I'd created structures that enabled me to get a good amount of distraction-free work done and to do what I want to do most rather than what I want to do now. After having completed the research for this book and writing the entire thing, I really do have a heck of a lot more power over my future because of the things I've covered in this book, and the process I had to go through in finding them.

What we all want is accomplishment. We want to improve. We want to prove that we're here for a *good* reason, and not just breathing in and breathing out for 80 years, but impacting those around us in a good and profound way. Discipline is one of the few things that is necessary for us to get what we want *most* in life. It's a necessity.

**We need discipline to achieve what we feel we're here to achieve, and we need accomplishment and freedom like we need air.**

We need accomplishment and freedom. We cannot go without them. We need accomplishment to feel as though we're here for a reason. If we live this life having accomplished nothing, regret will be our bedmate as we take our final breath. We need freedom to live on our terms, to feel as if we had some command and control over our existence. Both are not just *nice* to have in life, they're necessities, and pursuing them isn't only good, it's a duty.

This is especially true for men. We need freedom because we need to feel as though we have some control, some power, that we're not being held back or held down or suppressed. Men will fight and die for liberty, regardless of whether their so-called quality of life will be better with or without it. That is, a man would rather exist in uncertainty and be free, than have everything paid for and covered, and not be free. We need to be able to determine our future, and own the consequences of our actions. Without discipline we cannot be free. Without discipline we cannot achieve.

If you want more freedom and accomplishment, meaning and purpose, money and power, peace and happiness; are not so delusional as to think they're the product of luck or a handout; and instead understand that **what you want in life depends on who you are and what you do every day**, the *The Lost Art of Discipline* is your book. It will help you break down the most important barrier between you and your ideal existence: a lack of discipline.

You're not more likely to develop discipline if you're born wealthy or poor. You're not more likely to develop discipline if you're fat, skinny, jacked, or ripped. Acquiring discipline is completely under your control and has nothing to do with your past. My job with this book is to make that quest simple, so you're unbound by clutter and liberated by clarity.

> *Self-respect is the fruit of discipline; the sense of dignity grows with the ability to say no to oneself.*
>
> —*Abraham Heschel*

People who care about their lives—how they live and where they want to take themselves—have discipline.

The topic of discipline inspires many people to think only of strictness and limitation and of stiff, subdued conversation. That couldn't be farther from the truth.

Discipline gives us the freedom to unleash whatever power,

imagination, ambition, audacity, and daring we've kept within us. No more sedated goals, mediocre attempts, or safe aspirations.

Routine and habits are necessary but it cannot not solely be in pursuit of the mundane. Life, with all of its danger, opulence, audacity, and adventure, is not to be lived in safety. The nature of improvement dictates that we put ourselves in uncomfortable situations, aspiring to achieve things we don't know we can achieve.

If you want a safe way to get what you want from life, what you want from life isn't big enough, bold enough, or worthy of the potential you've been blessed with. Surely you have more to give, to gain, to chase.

American rapper The Notorious B.I.G. said, "mo' money, mo' problems," a statement that can only be true if one lacks discipline.

Let's discover how to amass money, gain meaning and purpose, build muscles and ideal bodies, and generally achieve success in all facets of our lives devoid of the problems that stem from the absence of discipline.

# CHAPTER 1
# Daring Discipline

*Far better is it to dare mighty things, to win glorious
triumphs, even though checkered by failure, than
to rank with those poor spirits who neither enjoy
nor suffer much, because they live in the gray
twilight that knows not victory nor defeat.*

—*Theodore Roosevelt*

Most of us go through life thinking that we're some day going to
magically rise to the occasion and build the life we want to build.

It's a myth. There's no such thing as a switch that you can turn
on to rise to the occasion.

This is something I always thought I had in my back pocket.
I thought that, eventually, I'd turn into the guy I wanted to be or
the guy that my goals and dreams needed me to become.

Boxing and business taught me otherwise. Boxing is often used
by good men to get rambunctious and possibly troubled young
men off the streets and into the ring. It provides undisciplined

youth structure, challenge, humility, and a productive place to focus their extra energy and anger.

The first time I walked into a boxing gym I was a tad apprehensive. I walked down the cracked concrete stairs to the sound of speed bags, heavy bags, and clanging chains into an underground world that smelled of sweat and blood and asbestos. And, as a young man, I discovered discipline.

What propelled me to begin boxing? I needed a sport. I needed structure and pain and the endorphins that are released from exercise that I couldn't get from working out to look good. I needed competition after a year off from playing college basketball to nurse a nagging injury. I needed struggle. I needed the physical adversity that's lacking from much of the work we find ourselves doing in today's 'evolved' society.

Boxing is a powerful sport. You develop discipline by putting your body through pain in the form of drills, roadwork, rope work, bag work, weight lifting, and so on. Then you're shown how little discipline you have by your multiple failures in the ring, be they caused by a lack of physical discipline or mental or the intertwining of both.

If you're talented in the sport but lack discipline, you're reminded of your deficiency toward the end of a round or late in a sparring session when you gas out but your opponent or sparring partner doesn't. He can't go easy on you because you're too tired to throw or slip or block a punch. Boxing isn't a compassionate sport. Sure, there's honor and sportsmanship, but the goal is to beat the other man up as viciously and scientifically as possible and to not stop until he either quits or can't physically continue.

If an opponent or sparring partner *did* go easy on you as you gasp for breath, pulling punches or even slapping instead of punching at full power or speed, he'd be doing you a disservice. By not teaching you the consequences of your lack of discipline in the form of a right cross or a crippling left hook to the body, he would allow you to live the illusion that you're not flawed, only pushing back the date when those lessons will inevitably be learned. And it's far better to learn those lessons incrementally in sparring, wearing 16 ounce gloves rather than 8 or 10 ounce gloves, and headgear.

**Lessons are taught in boxing by pain.**

Without pain, the lessons aren't learned, and if lessons aren't learned you don't improve. The same goes for life, when we're growing up and into adulthood. We learn what to do by winning, and we learn what not to do by failing. To not allow someone to do the wrong things, therefore, robs them of the teaching that will help them evolve into someone better. Too many soft people and parents do just that, they don't teach through *both* negative and positive rewards, only applauding the good and making excuses for the bad, and end up creating horrible, weak adults.

When we're not allowed to feel the sting and pain of failure, the crush of defeat that can bring us to the brink, we do not know what we can withstand, nor do we truly understand what we need to stop doing.

Pain, in boxing, is the immediate consequence. In life we often have to wait months or years or decades to see the consequences for our lack of discipline. In boxing it happens in seconds, and it happens frequently thereafter.

It's a perfect microcosm for life. It's similar to a regular gym, where we get stronger and leaner and more powerful by putting our body through pain. Except, in boxing, if you don't learn the lessons and do the work, rising early to run or staying late to remedy weaknesses, someone will show you your lack of discipline by kicking your arse.

Boxing teaches you discipline through the pain of effort and the pain of consequence. It shows you the necessity of routine and of habit. It also teaches you how to think in a disciplined manner, and the all-important discipline of humility, which I'd learn with one haymaker punch that landed perfectly on my then beardless chin.

I was a member of a couple boxing gyms. The first was good. I learned a lot about how to throw each punch and what techniques to use, but the guy who ran the gym was a fraud in the sense that he wasn't licensed to get me an actual fight. He knew way more about boxing than I did or currently do, but he kept pushing my fight date back until I finally got wise to what he was doing and left his gym.

I loved the sport and I wanted to fight, so I searched and asked around for a gym that actually had a fight team and sent their fighters to tournaments and even the Olympics. Thus, the second gym I joined was a fighter's gym. We'd travel around the city every month to spar with guys from other gyms. It was a way to face guys different from - and in some cases better than - the fellas we sparred with daily and grew to know intimately, both when they'd quit, their style, and where they were weakest. This 'fresh blood', in every sense of the term, was necessary to progress as a fighter.

After a few months at this second gym I was getting a lot better. I was putting my punches together, gaining confidence by the round. And even though I lost my first fight by decision, it was to a guy who'd already had eight or ten fights at a higher weight class, so I wasn't crushed. It was a part of the process, and winning the last round against a guy who was a good bit bigger than me gave me confidence, as did the countless hours of sparring and training.

I was getting loose, my punches were starting to flow. I was getting quicker. I was better able to anticipate what my opponent was about to do. Better yet, I was able to set him up and guide him to do what *I wanted him to do.*

I had more fights and won the next few and was really becoming confident with how I was fighting. I was disciplined in my routine. My habits were set in stone. I didn't miss a run or a training session. I was in the gym five to seven times a week like clockwork, and I stayed within my preferred weight range, so my diet was on point as well.

But I was getting cocky. And boxing makes no allowance for flagging discipline, physical or mental. In boxing, cockyness is blindness, it makes you unaware of the dangers that are to come. It allows you to let your guard down by way of arrogance that nothing bad will happen as a result.

Our gym scheduled an exhibition fight with another gym. I'd sparred before with the guy I was fighting and had dominated him. And I'm not just saying *dominated*; it was easy, too easy, so easy that I had no fear getting into the ring with him. As experience was about to teach me, I needed the edge that fear would have given me because without it I left myself open to the haymaker he threw that dropped me, and resulted in my compassionate cornerman stopping the fight.

I walked into the gym that day with an overabundance of confidence, convinced that I was going to knock my opponent out and looking only for the knockout. I wasn't setting anything up. I wasn't tricking him or changing up the speed of my punches. I was throwing haymakers, which leave you open to unexpected and unseen counterpunches.

I walked out of the gym that day with a headache, my eyes sensitive to sunlight, my pride beaten as much as my brain. But I had a wonderful lesson in hand:

*Discipline your body to be able to perform as you need it to, your mind to be able to attach itself to the right decisions and thought patterns, and your habits to enable to you thrive without being bogged down by the sea of unnecessary tasks we can follow in the run of a day.*

## Discipline is the power to do what is best instead of what is desired.

The battle isn't real.

Every moment we face two often opposing forces: what we desire right now versus what is best for us to do in the moment. The truth is, there is only what is best. What we desire in the moment is a myth.

While writing this book and particularly this paragraph, I searched online for a Benjamin Franklin quote. This led me to a website that sells prints and posters and lighters. I wanted the Zippo it offered with a cool quote on it.

I'd seen Zippos in Bond films and in Eastwood's movies. My desire for this Zippo was an illusion out of line with my greater goal. It was not influenced by what I truly want in life but by the films and fictions I had allowed society to thrust into my mind.

To win the battle between what in the moment you desire and what is best to do for your life requires that you have virtues that guide your life. Without guiding rules aligned with your overall values and views for what you want from life and the kind of person you want to be and how you want to live, you have no boundaries and are forced to make daily decisions without a framework or a singular purpose. You must consciously think about whether what you do is best for what you want and who you want to be or merely the desired illusion of marketing (purposeful or not).

Virtues, which we'll cover in more depth later, make the battle between your desires and purpose easy, simple, and clear. We need clarity. We do not need to spend our time and energy trying to figure out what's true and what isn't. We have more important things to do and work on.

Discipline, to a large degree, is simply:

**Living and thinking in a way that is in line with what we most want in life.**

**Doing the right things and avoiding the wrong things.**

The issue is that we don't always know what the wrong things are or what the right things are. To compound the problem, most of us lack the discipline and the courage to act on the right things and avoid the wrong things.

This isn't necessarily our fault. Our brains are ancient. They're evolved for such struggles as survival and not necessarily for the quest for self-improvement or to do the hard work that doesn't yield immediate results, like writing a book or building a business.

We're also conditioned today to believe that our desires are true and aligned with who we are at our core. This simplistic belief ensures a life of dependence, poverty, and slothfulness.

Think about your desires. Sometimes you want to kill the person who cut you off or eat an entire tub of ice cream or grab the butt of the cutie who just glanced at you on the street. Sometimes you want to sleep all day. Other times you want to leave your responsibilities and never return. Desires in the moment are not who you are. They're especially not a part of who you want to become, the man that will help you earn the life that you want most to live.

Where far too many people fail is in thinking that the gap between who they want to become—this ideal they've set for themselves and dreamt about—and who they are has to be closed over time. That's the wrong way to look at success, and one that will leave its attainment forever in the future, dependent on a milestone, not on you, **the individual who either is or is not successful.** Success, no matter how you define it, just like happiness, occurs. It happens. It is something you are or are not. Time rarely brings you closer to success if you are not acting successful everyday.

The characteristics of the person you desire to become govern how you must act in the moment. You must determine the actions of this man and live them daily. Then what you want, what this warrior will achieve, will come to you or you will eventually hunt it down.

This is discipline.

Discipline is doing the things that this future self would do while avoiding the things that he wouldn't do: the laziness, the envious thinking, the cheating, the weakness. Discipline is living greatly and daring to do so consistently.

The term 'greatness' is thrown around like a $2 whore. It's used and abused and its over-use makes it seem trivial, cliche. Deep down we all think 'greatness' is something for historical figures, it's a thing of the past or something only a pre-ordained few among us can have. We ignore the fact that any man can *live greatly*. We do not need permission to live in a great fashion, to dare mighty things, to aim higher than any man before us. Living greatly is merely a choice to act in a certain fashion and avoid acting as the masses do as they do mediocre work and fight over mediocre spoils.

Greatness is a legitimate goal, and acting in such a fashion is a choice any one of us can make.

You can do this, equipped especially with the tactics in this book. And you don't have to push greatness and success into the future. You can live greatly and successfully today by defining your ideal and disciplining yourself to live by it, in audacity of action and of thought. Just be disciplined in emulating the habits of your ideal self, and you become that ideal self in the present.

One of the myths about discipline is that it's for the meek, for those who want less rather than more. Discipline is not poverty. It is a lack of dependence on anything, the feeling that you need to keep up with the Jones', or the dependence on others for a handout. It is not modest living or quiet existence, unless, of course, you choose either or both. There is no power in doing what you have to do. That isn't not discipline.

Each is virtuous, but only if it's a choice. **It is not virtuous for a man to be peaceful if he does not have the capacity to be barbaric and dangerous. In the same way, it is not virtuous for a man to be frugal and poor if he has no other choice.**

The very nature of being disciplined enables you to become something better than what you currently are.

Throughout this book, we'll look at examples of how discipline propelled men to greatness, not goodness or mediocrity, but greatness.

While the undisciplined others in society slide into the existence they think they should be living or has been preordained for them, you need to develop the discipline to open yourself up to a new way of living, devoid of dependence, addiction, or the crippling fear that keeps men living small lives. Discipline frees you to reach your potential, to chase your dreams, to slay your demons.

## Define Victory

A few years ago, I read *The Rise of Napoleon Bonaparte* by David Asprey.

The average human hears the name Napoleon and thinks only of two things:

1.  His height.

2.  His ambition.

Before I learned about the man by reading that wonderful book, I thought of him solely as a power hungry person compensating for where he was born, for the subjugation of his birth nation, and for his short stature. I assumed, too, that Napoleon had grandiose dreams from the outset and pursued them ruthlessly.

The truth, however, resembles other stories of greatness and power. Napoleon didn't begin life with a desire to conquer the known world. He sought merely to better himself and his position in the world.

Think about his incredible rise to and the sheer audacity with which he chased power in the light of his beginnings. Imagine becoming the most powerful man in the world by becoming the emperor of the nation that conquered your nation. That would be like an Indian becoming the prime minister or king of England at the beginning of the twentieth century or like a Pole rising to rule the Soviet Union during the communist bloc era. It's so unlikely that it's hard to fathom, but that's what Napoleon did.

Napoleon was born on the island of Corsica, not in France. The French had conquered his homeland, and his first language was closer to Italian than French. At a time when birthplace, birthright, and language determined your place in the world, Napoleon was at a decided disadvantage. To acquire power—even to serve as an officer in the French army—required the right pedigree. Who you were born to, the last name you were either blessed or cursed with at birth, determined who you were to be for the remainder of your life.

Many today *feel* like their life is determined for them at birth, but as with many feelings, this one's a betrayal of the truth as examples of upward and downward mobility within society are plenty. In Napoleon's time, however, this *was the* truth.

Though success in Napoleon's life was a long shot given his birthplace, absent a few breaks, Napoleon might be unknown to history. At age ten, he and his older brother, Joseph, were allowed to enter French schools for aristocrats. In 1779, he was sent to the College of Autun in Burgundy, France, before transferring to the College of Brienne.

Both were French military schools whose students were of the French elite. Napoleon, an immigrant whose very nationality was questionable given France's conquest of his homeland, lacked all standing in French society for that reason and for his lack of title. The other students ridiculed him as a result.

**Napoleon did what others did not do
because they did not have to.**

Napoleon had a deep hate for his peers who'd fallen into wealth and power and position simply because of the womb they came out of. He hated how they partied and drank. This isn't an uncommon feeling many have toward those born with a silver spoon, but most simply let it eat away at them. They use it as an excuse not to work because they weren't given the same benefits as their wealthy peers so why work? The common sentiment today seems to be:

**Why work at all if others have a head start?**

What a cop out. What a weak way of looking at life, and while Napoleon *did* despise those who wasted their birthright in life partying and drinking, he still understood that only hard work and discipline would allow him to achieve the grandeur that he wanted to achieve. He couldn't ask a family friend for a favor, nor could he fall back on his family name. He had to be better than everyone. That, and that alone, was the only way he would win the victory in life he craved.

While his classmates drank and chased women, his nightly date was with the library and the sheer volume of knowledge she contained within her. He would read and study. While most fret over what they cannot control, like where they were born or the life they were born to, there are a minority who will not concern themselves with what they *cannot control*, and instead choose to focus only on what they *can control*. By focusing on what they can control they will not only accomplish much more than their envious and useless counterparts, but they will enjoy life, they will appreciate more and envy less. **They will be consumed not by bitterness but by ambition, the calling of their souls to prove that they were here for a good reason.**

Rather than wallowing in pity at his station in life or being consumed by the envy that claims far too many lives before they give themselves the chance to truly life, Napoleon did the only thing he could do to get what he wanted, **he worked harder than everyone else**. That was his reality. He could not change it any more than you or I can change ours.

Whether you think you'll be successful or unsuccessful, you're going to prove yourself right.

If you believe that your obstacles are unfair, you're going to act accordingly. Pity your status and bemoan the family that you were born into or don't have, and you're going to give up because you *believe* that you have a valid reason to do so.

You may not know exactly what your victory looks like - Napoleon certainly had no idea what he was destined for in life. But that must not prevent you from developing the habits daily that will bring you closer to even your vaguest notion of your ideal you.

Study any great man or woman, and what you'll find is discipline of action and of thought. **They did not act in a way that** betrayed what they wanted to achieve or who they wanted to become.

They developed the discipline to ignore the negative thoughts that can so easily claim a life once filled with promise. They developed the discipline to act in accordance with their ambitions, waking earlier, working harder and smarter, and staying truer to the course than others, who allowed discouragement and failure to derail them.

Throughout this book, we'll look at ways to become disciplined in thought and in action so that you too can win. And win you must. You're not here to exist, it's a waste of this gift of life to not improve, to not gain, grow, and win.

## Discipline Equals Freedom

*Freedom isn't secured by filling up on your heart's desire but by removing your desire.*

*—Epictetus*

Our view of discipline is often of the disciplinarian, not the millionaire or billionaire, the adventurer, or the warrior defending freedom in a hostile land.

Forget about the disciplinarian. Focus on the freedom. You may think that your adventures have to be put on hold because you're focused on discipline, but that's far from the truth. The truth is that discipline brings freedom into your life in a myriad of forms, including financial freedom to live how you want and the free time to pursue what you want and to travel where and when you want.

## Capacity

The fitter and healthier you are, the more you can do. A fat fella can't hike a mountain. A weak fella can't fight a bad guy. A tired fella can't work all day and have energy to play with his kids before bedtime and then resume work nightly.

Increased capacity in strength, conditioning, and energy, like martial arts, is mastered through discipline. By living a disciplined life, you open yourself up to more opportunity in every sense.

Life isn't fun when you're broke and in debt. The fastest path to financial freedom is to make more money and to spend less money on crap you don't need. Both are achieved through discipline.

The examples are endless. The scenarios never cease. Discipline liberates you from whatever holds you back. Whether it's fear, obesity, poverty, timidity, or a lack of ambition, discipline provides the path to freedom.

## Time

Free time should be scheduled and abundant. Yes, as an ambitious human you're going to work a lot, but working a lot and getting a lot done don't always align. Discipline enables you to get a lot done in less time. This allows you to have more fun and to explore more during your week.

I've been busy, and I've been efficient. They don't go hand in hand. Being busy is a state that our society praises, but it's efficiency that gets us the results we need.

Discipline allows you to stop being busy and ensures that you get more done more quickly. At first, you'll feel a little guilty with all of the free time you have to do the things you love, including spending quality time with loved ones. That will pass. When you see how much more you're achieving, your stress level will lower and your sense of accomplishment will rise.

Discipline is the giver of time, quality time, which will bring you the freedom to live the life you want to live, not the life that society expects of you.

## Money

The undisciplined man has the weight of debt on him. He can't do what he wants because he's spent money on things he desired in the moment but didn't align with his overall goal for his life - and often these desires in the moment take us *further away* from where we eventually want to be. He cannot do what he's bred to do either, because he's constantly going to be trapped by worry if he fails to get his house in order.

You're bred to win, whether you're born into poverty or wealth. You're bred to be a man, too, even if you lacked the guidance of a good father and role model. It's in your DNA to aspire to manhood, and to be a successful one at that. The fact that you're here means that you're a part of a long line of survivors. Maybe there are kings and conquerors in your line. At the very least there are hunters and warriors, men who bore children and provided the food and security they needed to grow to do the same.

You are not here to merely exist. You are here to thrive. And whether you or I like it or not, money plays *some* role in your victory.

Fiscal discipline is nearly a lost art. It's no longer expected that a man is good with his money as spending on desires in the moment has all but taken the place of sound fiscal values in the value-hierarchy of our society. And the importance of money cannot be discounted. We all want more of it. Money magnifies who you are.

If you're a prick, you'll be even more of a prick if you become rich. You'll have more resources than ever to conduct yourself badly. If you're generous, increased wealth will magnify your impact. As a man, money is especially important to you because your family needs financial security. Your wife wants someone she can depend on, someone whose earnings allow her the freedom from financial stress to be who she desires to be and to care for your family. Let's cut the crap, she isn't merely after love and emotion, she wants a symbiotic relationship, not a buddy. You're the man, the bread-winner, and as such, you can't be loose or irresponsible with that which you earn, no matter how much or how little you bring in. Crisis will come, and if you haven't sacrificed your desires in the moment for the overall welfare of your clan, you're going to add not only to your stress, but to the stress and uncertainty placed on them as well.

We're starting to deny this in modern society where we don't want to confine people to 'archaic roles', but when men have been hunting and gathering, defending, protecting, and presiding for hundreds and thousands of years, to ignore what's branded into our existence is to rip from men the *need* to protect someone, provide for someone, and as Ryan Michler of the Order of Man podcast says, preside over what's his. And this is a need. A man needs a castle like he needs meaning and purpose. He can live without each, but to give some proof that he's here for a reason - and proof to himself, not anyone else - some kind of responsibility over others is a must.

Finances are a simple way to measure how good you are at what you do, but only in terms of the wealth and power you culti-vate, and how much you earn in relation to the rest of your indus-try. The stuff you own does not add to your worth and often takes *away* the power you crave (and power can be defined however you want to define it, whether it's freedom, safety, impact, and so forth).

Too often the things we own end up owning us. If you've ever moved, you'll realize how much crap you own that you don't need, but because you've given something of value for it (money), you feel as though you *have to* keep it. It owns a piece of your space, a place in your castle, and you feel a connection to it, a debt to it that can't be shaken.

Discipline with money is understanding what you need, want, and what's merely a momentary desire and does not need to be acted upon. It is budgeting, investing, and structuring your time so you maximize your work in quality and quantity.

Money is where many lack the most discipline, and often don't care to change their bad habits because it hasn't yet gotten *bad enough* to do so. A lack of money can also hurt other areas of your life, be they relationships, or your sense of meaning, purpose, and accomplishment, and the amount of unnecessary stress you carry because your finances are in an unnecessary horrible state.

*Making money* is great and good and something you should aim to do more of. But if you've read *The Millionaire Next Door*, you'll know a few things about money:

1.  It's as much about how you use it and where you put it as it is about how much you bring in. If you abuse the money you make, spending frivolously and stupidly, what makes you think you'll change if you make more of it? Indebtedness is a constant at every income level.

2.  The power of compounding is as or more important than the power of earning. If you make an okay living, it grants you the potential to be wealthy.

3.  Most millionaires in America don't own fancy cars or homes. Avoiding ostentatious trappings is why they're millionaires. This is discipline. They don't do what everyone else does because they have more important fish to

fry and bigger ideas of what they want from life. They, for example, want freedom over image and social status.

Wealthy people invest first and spend next. Broke people spend first and if there's anything left, *then* they'll invest it, or they don't invest at all and they just spend.

Many of the people in the big homes and the costly cars lack discipline and enter their retirement years carrying a lot of debt. And they have no clue how they're going to survive if they can no longer work.

We'll take the approach of the millionaire, not the fella trying to show everyone that he's important or valuable by buying things he can't afford. We'll enjoy discovering financial freedom and avoid being strangled by debt or dependent on someone else for sustenance. We'll free ourselves from desires that aren't true to who we genuinely want to be and the most ambitious idea we have for the kind of life we want to live.

We'll opt for power and freedom rather than the suffocating stress of being in debt or trying to impress others with what we own. The former are virtuous and good pursuits, while aiming to show how much you have is fruitless, it brings only sorrow and pain and it takes *away* meaning from one's life.

## Peace

*How satisfying it is to dismiss and block out
any upsetting or foreign impression, and
immediately to have peace in all things.*

—*Marcus Aurelius*

Discipline is doing the right things and not doing the things that hurt you or hold you back from living the life you want to live.

Discipline gives you peace through the freedom to do what you love and what feeds your soul and your very being and to not do anything contrary. If you're not doing what you love, but doing something *for those who you love*, the freedom is the same.

Discipline gives you the freedom to struggle toward something great rather than out of something horrible and self-imposed.

Discipline is freedom from your porn addiction, your shopping addiction, your drug addiction, and your inability to save or decipher what you want instead of what someone else wants for you. A disciplined life is a peaceful life. You know what you have to do, and you do it. You know what you must not do, and you don't do it. By day's end, you're satisfied, calm, and at peace with your life.

*To a disciplined mind there is always only one thing, that which demands their attention in the present. Nothing else is allowed to exist. This is peace.*

Most people repeatedly do what keeps them small. These habits are not propelling them toward something better, only digging them into a deep hole of despair, self-loathing, pity, regret, and envy.

A life without discipline is a cancerous existence. A life of discipline is peaceful. And while we talk at length about accomplishment and achievement, what we're really after, or an aspect of what we really want, is peace.

We want to be at peace, comfortable with our thoughts, proud of who we are and what we're doing, and free of the guilt that comes from addiction or the stress that comes from debt or the worry that many of us live with.

Discipline gives you peace. It is an escape from worry and fear and being less than you can be.

# Purpose

Live with purpose. Avoid the accidental lives that too many live. As crazy as the questions are: *Is there a reason for what you do daily? Does each of your actions during the day take you down a path toward improving your life?*

Simply by engaging in honest work, there is purpose to your day. And the more you engage in good, honest work without distraction in thought or following a link that leads you to a video-watching binge, the more meaning you're inevitably going to have in your life.

The feeling of doing good work is far more powerful than we want it to be. We want the answer to the meaning of life to be found in something grand, different, even dangerous, when life's meaning is as much about doing honest work well as it is about some experience that will last moments and create nothing. The actual work doesn't matter, doing it well and with pride, does.

Discipline gives you the freedom to ignore the actions that don't feed your purpose in life, that don't propel you forward, even if that forward movement is so incremental it's difficult to notice it as movement at all (writing a book is a good example of this as I'll get a handful of pages done in a day only to have to go back and edit the crap out of those pages about a dozen times after they've been written, and the work that's being done is only finally held in my hand a year later and maybe, just maybe, the result of the work isn't even a success, so the time and effort feels even more static, though I know deep down it isn't).

What I've realized is that the work must get done, and by doing the work my life has more meaning, regardless of its result. That said, if I lack discipline in doing the work, if I fail to focus on a single task at a time and instead jump from project to project, I end the day feeling as if I've failed. I write this because in talking with other humans I see this as a constant. When we're fully engaged in something we feel good, proud, we stop thinking about things that lead us to worry or bring us stress and we simply do what's in front of us.

The opposite of that singular focus on work brings us that worry and stress that has a snowball effect on both our minds, our quality of life, and when we worry and stress we tend to try to do everything at once rather than the single thing that should command our attention.

Being busy on more than one tasks stresses us out because we *try* to do a lot but in reality get very little done. Focusing on the work relieves us of stress while also making us feel a sense of pride and a connection with the work. Yet, when we worry and stress we tend to do the former - focusing on everything without doing anything - in turn, creating more of that stress and worry we're trying to avoid.

I just had this happen.

I had planned on working on this book for 3 hours. But I also had the responsibility of trying to figure out what I was going to do with my lady after the work day. On top of that there were 3 other tasks I was aiming to have finished by day's end. Sitting down to write, I couldn't get the nagging responsibility of the date I had to plan later in the evening. I had to finish a bit early, I concluded, so I could plan that and clean the house, which led me to not only work on this book, but open up the web site back end to edit an article, check my phone to communicate with my support team to settle some issues with a promotion that we just ran, and do research on a new web site theme - that last one didn't even need to be done, it was a made-up task added to the other slough of tasks that yielded zero results. I finally caught myself in what I was doing. I shut the computer off, grabbed a book, regrouped, restructured the day, read, then stopped, set a timer, and started back on the book in a completely new 'window', blocking all other windows on the computer from being able to be viewed.

The simplicity of focusing on a single task has a profound effect not only in that we accomplish more, but that we feel better by doing fewer things at a time.

Busyness yields very little in the way of results, while disciplined focus produces greater results and a much more powerful feeling of pride and accomplishment, a deeper connection to the work.

We each have something worthwhile to pursue in our lives. We have work, which is a worthwhile endeavor, and then we have the hobbies and pursuits outside of work that also need to be worthwhile.

Whether you're here on this planet for a good reason or not is an entirely personal choice. The universe, society, your family, they do not get to decide this for you. While your Maker *may have intended* to put you here for a reason, your parents the same, only you can choose if you *are* here for a reason or not.

**You create such meaning, purpose, and reason for life by doing things worth doing.**

One of the most common questions I'm asked on my website is about purpose and the lack thereof. It's asked by young and older guys alike; they all struggle with purpose. They don't know what direction to set theirs sails or where to focus their talent and effort.

In his book, *Resilience*, Eric Greitens, a former navy SEAL and now the governor of Missouri, talks about the issue of soldiers returning home from the hyper-focused environment of battle, where the mission is so clear. Soldiers have only to focus on their role in fulfilling an objective. Home life is different. The options are endless, and even more-so today than ever before. People frequently change careers and college majors in a search for the right one. Finding a purpose isn't as simple as it once was, and returning military personnel often falter for lack of clear objectives.

When our purpose is clear, we wake every day knowing that we're needed, that people depend on us, that we have things to do. Without a clear purpose because we've failed to define it, we wander. And humans aren't meant to wander aimlessly, **we need a challenge.**

You give *yourself* that ideal to strive for, that purpose for being, by *choosing* what to pursue, what to work on, who you want to become. Life does not hand us a purpose, though it often falls into our laps in the form of an interest or a job that intrigues us, that challenges us to learn it, become better at it, and succeed at it.

## Where You Should Already Be

*A disciplined mind leads to happiness, and*
*an undisciplined mind leads to suffering.*

—*Dalai Lama XIV*

Discipline is efficiency. It enables you to get things done in a better, faster manner without getting sidetracked. Develop discipline, and you become more effective. You become more productive. **Logically, this should lead to our knowing that the sooner we develop discipline in our lives the faster we'll achieve what we want to achieve and become who we want to become.**

What if you'd developed such discipline five years ago?

We're told that we shouldn't regret things, that we should accept what's happened and move forward. However, if you don't deeply feel your missed opportunities you're not going to be aware of them in the future and you're not going to be the man who can take advantage of them when they cross your path.

This pain is good. Be in it. Use it. Use the pain of regret, the understanding that you could already be far more successful than you are right now, to do what must be done now, so your future doesn't hold the same pain.

This is a matter of understanding that your time here is limited, that you're dying, that with each breath you have one less breath left. And up to this point, you've wasted a hell of a lot of time.

You could be better. You could have more money, more freedom, more pride in who you are, a deeper purpose, a more profound meaning. You could be walking this Earth as the man you are in your dreams, doing the big things, with the strength and grit and will to make a real impact, not just on your own life but on the lives of those around you, including people you don't know.

Again, I'm writing this as much to myself as to you. We're all in the same boat. I've pissed away so much time and money, the recollection of which is like a weight tied to my ankles as I try to swim to the surface. We're all wastrels. Each one of us is short of where we could be. For the warrior, this is encouraging. There's room to grow. There's a challenge ahead. No matter where you are there's light in your future.

You're nowhere near your potential. You haven't come close to realizing what you're capable of. It sucks to realize this. Think of where you are. Now think of where you'd ideally like to be in this very moment.

Is it on your massive ranch or in your mansion or overlooking Lago di Como in the North of Italy with your sweetheart sitting beside you looking at you with adoring eyes?

Be there mentally. Put yourself in that dream scenario and then open your eyes and realize it could already be your reality if only you'd man up, think bigger, and have the balls to live a life that most people are unwilling to live—**of discipline and not desire.**

It hurts to think about opportunities wasted. It will hurt a million times more to be lying on your deathbed knowing you could have done more, knowing that it was a lack of something you had control over that led you to fail in life.

Imagine lying on your deathbed thinking about all that you didn't do. Yet, most people die with regret-filled hearts. Sure, there's love and happiness, but most of us lead lives that are but a fraction of what our potential suggested could have been our lives, all because we didn't think big enough and lacked focus and discipline and grit.

It doesn't matter where you start; no one cares. Where you end up is your responsibility. No matter where you're born it's an advantage. In a recent episode of Jerry Seinfeld's *Comedians in Cars Getting Coffee*, Jerry's guest, Tracy Morgan, talks about how impressive it is that Richard Pryor, the legendary comedian, did so well in comedy in spite of being born to a mother who was a prostitute, a father who was a pimp, and a grandmother who was a madame. Jerry says something so incredibly profound, "I think those things are all advantages."

This outlook doesn't have to be confined to comedy, where we make light of our shortcomings in life, and even our beginnings. No matter how we come into the world there's advantages to it. And discipline is how we realize these advantages.

The only thing that really gets in the way of us viewing our obstacles or experiences as anything *but* an advantage, is our modern access to everyone else in the form of social media. I'm sure we've always compared ourselves to others, but the 'others' could only be the fella with the cave or the hut next door, or the other farmer working the same field under the same lord who just happened to have a much better looking wife than we had.

Our comparisons, if they really existed at all in times when our survival was our primary focus, were few. Today, they're endless. And today we see only what the others want us to see, the images they want to show us. Taking pictures of the work, the toiling, the frustration, the persistent and consistent effort doesn't get 'likes', so people are rewarded when they show only the result of said work, and we look at what they have, where they are, what they've accomplished, and shit on our lives for our perceived deficiencies.

Be careful.

Your story is the only story you have. Your history is the only foundation you have to build upon. You cannot change what was, you can only craft what will be.

Take pride in where you've come from even if it's a horrible place, because turning that horrible place into something grand is truly something to be proud of.

# CHAPTER 2
# Myths That Make Men Mediocre

*For the moment all discipline seems painful rather than pleasant, but later it yields the peaceful fruit of righteousness to those who have been trained by it.*

*—Hebrews 12:11*

On some level all we really want is control. We want to decide where our life goes and what we do with this single, brief experience. For the life of me, I can't figure out how to wield such control, where we point ourselves in a good, great, meaningful direction, without discipline.

Discipline is the literal focusing of your minutes and hours to an end that you deem good.

If, however, you don't believe that you can become who you want to become or achieve what you want to achieve, you won't develop the necessary discipline to live how you want. There are certain myths in our society that, if believed, keep people from living grand, flourishing lives because it gives them a perceived valid reason to not try at all, they make effort pointless.

> *Whether you think you can, or you*
> *think you can't—you're right.*
>
> —*Henry Ford*

There are success stories from every walk of life. Choose any of the most improbable among them as proof that you can do truly great things whether you're poor, middle class, rich, or anywhere in between, and you'll free yourself from the shackles that are disbelief and mediocrity claiming to keep you from living a life that you would deem as successful.

Much of it, if we're honest, is cynicism. It's not a cynical outlook that you've had since birth, but one you or I or anyone have been taught to have. We're fed only bad news. We're told only the crummy statistics that, over time, cloud our view over the world and what's possible.

Take this notion of the 1% in America. We're pitched it as a static group, but it isn't. Especially in societies that have more economic freedom, not those bogged down by regulation, the 1%, just like the Fortune 500, is incredibly fluid. We're told by intellectuals who've never actually put their money in the market and who *do* enjoy tenure, where their jobs are secure once they reach a certain point in their career and movement ceases, that this 1% is a club of sorts that will collude against the rest of us in society. It's just not true. These 'intellectuals' who seem to be obsessed with inequality don't actually have relationships with people in different classes. They're in a bubble, and they don't understand - or they gloss over - the fluidity between classes in places that enjoy the economic freedom that they seem to want to destroy. Their work doesn't have them produce things besides maybe a book or two and a few papers that don't benefit a soul, but divide much more than they bring together.

Due to the fact that it takes risk to make money in North America, especially, similar risk (or an aversion to it once that place in the 1% is achieved) often sends people who've reached that 1% back down to the top 5% or 50%.

In fact, over 10% of Americans will spend at least a year in the top 1%, and more than half of all Americans will spend a year in the top 10 percent, *and* only 10 percent of the wealthiest five hundred American people or dynasties were so thirty years ago.[1]

How powerful! We're fed this lie that the rich stay rich and the poor stay poor but we have a lot more control over our station in life, especially here in North America, than we'd seemingly like to admit.

These intellectuals and the media feed this growth in cynicism, and those who are 'seemingly' obsessed with income inequality want to adopt systems - like socialism or capitalism - that secure wealth for the few and make every other human in society equally mediocre.

The point is that this cynicism isn't founded on truth. Not only is it founded on a lie but on a lie that wants to solve the lie with another lie - the lie that the government deserves more control over one's life than the private citizen.

How we're raised also has a massive impact, but regardless of how well we were raised it can't act as an excuse for failure or for believe that failure is an inevitable outcome because at some point we have to take responsibility for our own lives - if, of course, we want to live them well.

I had a great upbringing. I was raised by wonderful parents

---

1 The last part was taken from Nassim Taleb's book, *Skin in the Game,* which should be read by everyone, along with his other books. We're fed a narrative that pits those who have a lot against those who don't quite have as much, yet most of us spend time having a lot and not having much at all. There's much more movement between the perceived classes than we're allowed to believe.

who backed me up and pushed me and supported me, and yet, *I can be cynical*, and in the past I've been very cynical.

I started life out thinking that anything was possible, but life chose to show me that this wasn't true. And then envy took root, and no matter what I had or accomplished, I saw that someone else had won, done, or accomplished something even better. And, I hated it.

I hated that, with seemingly less work, they earned far more money than me, often in a year than I had in my life. I hated that success seemed to come so easy to them and so difficult to me. I've been there.

I've pitied myself before. I've wished I was given a different brain or blessed with some damn talent in the realm of marketing or writing or this or that or whatever. It's all bullshit. You have to realize that it's bullshit or you doom yourself to a life clouded by a cynicism that isn't actually true.

People who make tons of money or simply achieve great successes do so because, in some form or another, they deserve it, and they usually deserve it by being disciplined in some form or another.

Maybe they've disciplined themselves to do the right things and not the wrong things. Maybe they don't chase every idea that pops into their skull. Maybe they structure their days so they get more work done, and they do this over a long period of time. And after years of doing great work they get their break and it seems like success has come in an instant, but the truth is that it came because they did the right things and avoided doing the wrong things over a long period of time.

They may work 8 hours a day, but they're great hours, far more efficient and effective than your 16 hours where you accomplish little but do a lot.

The point is that this cynicism held by so many is trained, and it needs to be unlearned. In the following chapter I'll give you examples of success that are far more unlikely than yours. You can see this, believe it, accept it and move forward with this truth, or you can remain cynical.

Actually, no you can't. This is *the truth*. The truth isn't debatable. If you are disciplined over a long enough period you'll improve your life. Simple. Use these examples as motivation. You do not need anymore proof. It's all around you. **Bad habits lead to failure; good habits lead to greatness.**

My opposition may be a worthy, strong, powerful adversary. The media, the education system, TV, music, even your family, may be unconsciously working to make you disbelieve that your success - even your life - and happiness is under your control. As such, I ask you to put the blinders on while you're reading this book. Let *it* influence you. If you allow it to, the worst thing that could happen is that you gain much more control over your life and how its lived, and the direction in which you point it.

## The Talent Myth

*Talent is insignificant. I know a lot of talented ruins. Beyond talent lie all the usual words: discipline, love, luck, but, most of all, endurance.*

—*James Baldwin*

We like stories of talented people with innate abilities. We like them because it means that greatness or success or mastery is born and not earned. It excuses us from giving our absolute best, from persisting and, at the end of the toiling and endless work, possibly failing.

Failure is always a possibility, though it's only an end if you allow it to be. The choice is to pursue your ideal in the form of work, or to not. To not is to give up, to be weak, to submit. Don't submit.

These stories of talented greats are fables. This belief that talent is the primary factor that helps people succeed is nonsense. Talent exists, and we should appreciate it, but if it's devoid of discipline it's useless. Where discipline and interest and passion exist in place of talent, victory is won, on an incredible scale.

**To use a lack of perceived talent as a reason to not give maximal effort is selling yourself, and the world and the people who would benefit from your work, short.**

While I'll show you that no matter the ideal, discipline will help you get there, you have to appreciate where you are in comparison to where you once were. Discipline will inevitably help you improve, but if you don't recognize the improvement it's all for naught.

That said, it's cynicism that holds the majority back from setting out on the path that their soul begs them to embark upon.

**The myth that talent is the deciding factor for success has led far too many people to avoid developing the discipline that their goals, dreams, and aspirations demand they develop because, from the point of view that talent is supremely important, discipline is useless.**

In his book *The Talent Code*, Daniel Coyle asks why hotbeds of talent have arisen throughout history and into the modern day and if it's really talent that creates cultures of greatness or something else entirely. He highlights the numerous legendary artists from Florence during the Renaissance; the many world-class soccer players from the same area in Brazil; and the profusion of world-class tennis players from a single, tiny, impoverished tennis club in Russia. What he found was that it wasn't talent at all but a combination of interest and practice— and, more so, a particular kind of practice—that led to so much prowess hailing from single sources.

Whether we're talking about da Vinci and Michelangelo or Ronaldo and Ronaldinho, how they learned and how much interest they had in their craft had more to do with their common rise than some genetic predisposition. Innate talent isn't the commonality for the ascension of talented groups of people.

Coyle posits that whether or not a person has talent and ability for accelerated learning and growth is not the result of a blessing or a curse, respectively. It instead is owed to something everyone has: myelin, which is essentially the muscle of the mind.

Acquiring proficiency in any skill results in and is the result of increased deposits of myelin. This fatty white substance surrounds the axons of some nerve cells, protecting and insulating them and enhancing their transmission of electrical impulses. When you learn something new, your myelin multiplies and compounds your ability to learn further.

Myelin is the biological effect of practice. What we see as talent or skill or innate ability to do something better than everyone else isn't a blessing or the result of a birth lottery. Michelangelo and da Vinci and Donatello weren't given divine talent that helped them acquire skill easier and faster than everyone else. They and the other artistic geniuses who flourished in Florence during the Renaissance benefited from the body's reaction to deep, purposeful practice: added myelin.

Levels of proficiency depend entirely on how you practice. **To develop skill, or talent as some refer to it, struggle must take place.** There is no other way to improve and to get your skill circuits to fire and perform optimally than to extend yourself, to make mistakes, to learn from those mistakes, and to allow your brain to adjust and grow. The more intense this struggle, the greater the learning.

Earlier, I called myelin the muscle of the mind. Like muscle, **it grows under tension and regresses under ease.** If you stop working out, your muscles atrophy. They need deep, purposeful work, as does your mind. Mind and muscle alike also need to be confronted with new challenges. Your reach must continually exceed your grasp. Mastery of a skill—be it shooting a basketball, writing, painting, sculpting, playing tennis, archery, investing, marketing, selling, or the like—isn't an opportunity that only a few hold the key to.

You are not born with the talent to learn a skill easier and faster than others. The way you learn may be different. An intense interest in a craft will probably cause you to focus more intently and practice longer and more deeply than someone else. But we all have myelin and the capacity to develop it.

To use a lack of innate talent as an excuse to fail is a self-fulfilling prophecy. If you believe you are not worthy enough of what you pursue, you will prove yourself correct. To change that belief, you have only to look at the evidence, to seek the truth.

Olympian and author Matthew Syed dives deep into the power of competition. He examines how competition and a supreme interest in a sport can create greatness where talent doesn't appear to exist.

One example he gives in his book, *Bounce,* is from his sport, table tennis. Syed recounts a time when members of England's table tennis team were tested for their reaction speed. Desmond Douglas, a top player renowned for his lightning reflexes, was oddly enough found to have the slowest reaction time. The result was so shocking that the machine used for testing was thought to be faulty. But the result was repeated time and time again. It made no sense to the experts or the athletes.

How did a guy with the slowest reaction time end up becoming one of the best table tennis players in the world and legendary for wildly fast hands?

The answer is anticipation, not naturally quick reflexes. And anticipation resulted from Douglas's deep practice of the game.

Douglas got so good at anticipating that he was reacting before his opposition completed a shot. As proven, his reflexes weren't great. But thousands of hours of purposeful practice helped him compensate and become a top player in a sport where fast reflexes would seem to be a necessity and, indeed, the difference between high-level competitors and the rest.

Douglas, thankfully, was ignorant of his lack of talent with respect to reaction time. He simply loved the sport and played and practiced it for hours. That intense interest and focus ensured that he overcame a seemingly insurmountable obstacle. A slow reaction in table tennis is akin to not being able to jump high in basketball, which brings us to Steve Nash.

Steve Nash is a great example of someone who pursued his interests instead of listening to people tell him that he wasn't anything near a prototypical basketball player. Who's Steve Nash?

Nash is a two-time NBA MVP, an eight-time NBA All-Star, a three-time selection to the All-NBA First Team, and more. He was a great player. Many in the know would put him on a revised Top-50 NBA Players of All Time list.

Nash, however, did not fit the profile of even an average NBA player and seemed an outlier to ever play in the NBA. He's from a small town in British Columbia, Canada, that had never produced an NBA player. Canada as whole only had a few players reach the NBA before he made it, and none of them came anywhere close to achieving what he achieved. But it wasn't as if he was a phenom. He had good but not spectacular athletic ability. And he wasn't exceptionally tall by NBA standards, at around six feet, three inches.

Pretty much everything about Nash, from how he looked

to his level of talent, screamed that his noteworthy achievement would be merely as a very good high school basketball player. What set him apart, however, was his degree of interest in basketball, his discipline, and his work ethic.

Nash's philosophy was to never miss a day of basketball training because missing one was an excuse to miss another and another after that and so on. It wasn't talent that led him to become one of the greatest point guards and among the greatest players of all time. If he'd believed that talent determined outcome, he never would have had the hunger and passion to achieve what he did.

Believing in innate talent is a choice. **You can choose to believe that it determines success as a rationale for your lack of success. Or you can choose not to limit your future with such a fallback excuse and allow yourself to succeed.**

Discipline is necessary for success. To succeed, you must apply discipline and choose to dispense of the many excuses seen as truths. Let go of the talent myth, and you'll free yourself from chains threatening to hold your life back.

You can believe the fables, if you choose, but you'll live with an excuse, a reason to not give your all. Consciously or subconsciously you'll believe you're not sufficiently talented or worthy of rising to what you aspire.

Listen, success of any kind is difficult, and it's near impossible if you have an excuse in your back pocket. You need to see the truth, that you have the talents to get what you want, all that you need is more discipline, and thank God, discipline is something that's completely under your control.

Michelangelo, an artistic genius on a level the world has rarely seen, is quoted as saying, "If people knew how hard I had to work to gain my mastery, it would not seem so wonderful at all."

The myth of talent keeps far too many perceived untalented

individuals from achieving what they have it within them to accomplish. When talent is real, when genius and God-given ability rule your perception of what it takes to accomplish anything of great value, you're excused from giving the effort required to achieve success. Rather, in *your own mind*, you're excused from said effort. The effort is required regardless, but the excuse gives you a reason not to try, and if you initially try, not to persist.

The truth is that you don't fall back on talent. You don't depend on abilities you're born with. In times of crisis, under the lights, in your big moment, you will only have your habits, your discipline, which is essentially the training you need to succeed in such a moment.

It's no different with life or business. **You cannot flip a switch and become something you haven't trained to be.** There's a reason why elite soldiers, martial artists, writers, and businessmen, etc., train so rigorously. The best are the best because of their training, their discipline, not because a fluke genetic predisposition enabled them to rise to the moment without ever preparing for the moment.

**You are a collection of your habits, and for good or bad, they will give you what you deserve.**

## Act Like a Winner

*Winners act like winners before they become winners. That's how they become winners.*

—*Bill Walsh*

There are a few important factors in the equation for achievement that need to be highlighted:

- Winners have an ideal. They have a goal. Humans need direction and know it or not are always going somewhere. It's best that you determine your somewhere and then align your habits with your chosen direction or you'll wander off the path and end up lost in a place completely unlike where you'd ideally want to be.

- Winners reduce the macro to the micro. They set their sights high and determine the daily habits they need to attain their daily, micro, goals.

Greatness, success, your dream is rarely a complicated thing to achieve. It's a problem you have to solve. The difficulty lies not in solving it but in failing to adhere long term to the habits that will solve it and make the dream reality.

If you do the right things for long enough, you will win. Nothing in the world, in fact, can then stop you from winning.

If you've ever maintained a set of good habits for a long period of time you'll know precisely what I'm talking about. There's a momentum that comes from consistency, and whether you're doing it on purpose or not, you're being consistent. You're either being consistently slothful or lazy, distracted and inefficient, or you're taking command of your habits and being consistently efficient, good, and effective.

The choices are so clearly defined. We're doing it anyway. We're doing *something*, yet so few don't take the time to think about and determine whether that something will bring them closer to their ideal, or further away. They allow the 'something' to happen to them, whether it's a phone call that breaks them from their work or the press of a button that turns into a two-hour television watching session.

You're always doing something. When you step back and take

command of your habits, your daily rituals and routines, you ensure that what you do is good, right, and true. It aligns with the direction you want to go.

Momentum is powerful.

I've witness it in my own life, where I maintain the correct habits and accomplish just enough work over a long enough period and realize that it's happening, that the business is growing, the books are being written and published and I'm seeing the results from my work.

It doesn't happen overnight, you just see it slowly occur in the data that measures success in the business.

Momentum also has the opposite effect.

I've capped periods of great work that grew the business to new levels, then got lazy, lost the habits that brought success, and though it took up to 6 months, the momentum of mediocrity sent the business heading in the opposite direction.

Whether you know it or not you're using momentum to push your life in a direction. If you're not in control of your habits, you're creating a snowball effect of debt, of a lack of accomplishment and enjoyment. Your business will fail, you'll acquire so much debt that it'll seem near impossible to pay off, and your relationships will suffer under the self-imposed stress you've placed on your entire life.

If you do take control of your habits, it may not seem like anything special is happening. You'll definitely feel better about yourself and who you are because you're doing good work and living well. Your soul feels right. But you still have bills to pay and the breaks don't seem like they're coming. Life feels normal, just with a bit less stress and worry.

And then things will start to happen that don't have explanation.

Victories occur that you didn't plan for.

I've gone through such a period recently and rather than changing my habits in times of plenty, the habits that won the times of plenty will remain.

When you act like a winner for a long enough period, when you do the things winners do, the victory comes.

## The Myth of the Birth Lottery

*The greatest heritage a man can have
is to be born into poverty.*

—*Andrew Carnegie*

You may believe, or you may have been taught to believe, that great achievements are the result of talent. It's convenient to think that way because it excuses you from doing the work you need to do to accomplish what you want to accomplish.

If success is achieved through winning the birth lottery, you can excuse yourself from the years of failure and anguish and constant pivots in strategy that high achievement demands of everyone. The pursuit of something greater, of excellence, is painful. It's the act of attempting to do what you cannot yet do. It's necessarily painful because it's the act of improvement, and not everyone is willing to go through this, so excuses like talent and nepotism preordained status become favorable to the struggle of forward movement. The flaw in this outlook is that the *end* and the journey of achievement is far better than the regret, pain, and indebtedness, that is earned when you never give anything everything you have to give it.

Having an excuse like the belief that success is something you're born into allows you to rationalize your failure rather than put out your best effort. It's a fallback that you rely on to justify taking fewer risks, giving slight effort, and not staying the course and persisting until you accomplish something.

The stories of Napoleon Bonaparte and Steve Nash illustrate that the idea of a birth lottery that determines your future by social class, parental quality, race, gender, innate talent, or whatever else you can come up with is utter nonsense. Even though they can be seen as helpful, they can also be detrimental. The man who doesn't have to work, often won't. And the man who has to work his entire life learns valuable lessons that are necessary for success that may not come naturally to the man who's seemingly given everything, but in reality given nothing.

To further this, your duty isn't to end your life better than anyone else, but to end your life better than when you started. That isn't a thing to applaud, but a duty, an expectation, and one that's lost in a society that pushes comparisons to others rather than an appreciation of one's own path.

Forget about where others started. Stay in your lane and finish your race in a better place, as a better person and a better man than you were or were expected to be with what you were given and who you were when you started.

> *"The greatest thing a man can possibly do in this world is to make the most possible out of the stuff that has been given him. This is success, and there is no other. It is not a question of what someone else can do or become which every youth should ask himself, but what can I do? How can I develop myself into the grandest possible manhood?"*
>
> *Orison Swett Marden*

When you begin to study history, and you begin to *look for* examples of men who've risen from situations like yours, mine, and much worse, you see proof in the power of disregarding things that everyone blindly believes, and simply doing the best with where you are and what you have.

Don't dismiss all but contemporary such tales as archaic and inapplicable to the modern day. Laud the many men of history who struggled against mightier odds than most of us face today to pull themselves up to great heights.

Every nation has ample examples of such people who achieved success by anyone's definition regardless of their origins. Choose to focus on these examples and not on the masses who remain small and insignificant as they hide behind excuses for doing little. Figures from history are especially admirable given the odds that they faced. Their chances of success were so much less likely than ours today.

Yet succeed they did. At a time when family status was the determiner of your future, **when the aristocracy jealously guarded against upstarts**, some very disciplined men rose above their stations and climbed the ladder of class to exceed their wildest dreams. If it could be done then, there's no bloody reason to excuse yourself from attempting a similar quest for greatness today. Think upon the likes of Napoleon and of James Cook.

Imagine being born into a farming family, as was Cook's lot, at a time when your father's profession dictated your own. Today, we merely *feel* as if our family origin is the determining factor on what we pursue and aim to achieve and where we end up in life. I have peers who were born rich and are useless, and I have friends who were born into the lower middle class and are now rich and getting richer. It's a factor, for sure, but you determine your life. Don't listen to anyone or anything that tells you otherwise. Now, in eighteenth-century England, it did have an impact and it did determine what you could pursue in life.

When James Cook was born, his life was laid out for him. His old man was a farmer, and not the owner of a farm, merely a farm worker. Today, if your dad is a farmer there's a chance you're going to be a farmer as well, but it's not a given the way it was in Cook's time (to ensure this isn't taken the wrong way, being a farmer is one of the best things a man can be, something that should be applauded and admired by the rest of society if it isn't already). In the 1700s, your future was almost exclusively determined by birth. Your class at birth determined your class at death. Rising from one class to another was almost unheard of, unlike today, when, with the elimination of most class structures, this kind of thing is commonplace, **especially among people with the discipline to do the right things for a long enough period.**

*Earlier I mentioned this myth that the 1% is static. Especially in North America and other places that have economic freedom, the 1% is fluid, just like the Fortune 500. People come and go from the 1%, and statistically, most people reading this book will spend at least 1 year in that 1% in their lifetime. During Cook's time the 1% was no fluid, it was static, and it was static because those in that 1% wanted to keep it so, and they had the titles and the structure to do so.*

This set-in-stone class structure makes Cook's story extraordinary. He rose above his class in spectacular fashion, choosing not just one path in life that differed from his father's but multiple paths, including the pursuit of adventure and glory, rather than money.

And his father was instrumental to his success. James Cook Sr. wasn't a landowner and had no share in farm profits, but he was the foreman of the largest farm, Airyholme, in Great Ayton. He consequently had stature in the town next only to landowners. **For many parents, the dream isn't to achieve wildly successful lives for themselves; it's to set up their kids up to do that, how admirable.** Cook senior's work ethic elevated him from farmhand to foreman and showed young James the value of hard work and perseverance. Lessons learned from the father facilitated the extraordinary life that the son would go on to live, becoming the world's most famous and arguably most successful explorer.

The explorer's mentality was fostered on the farm, amid his family's subservience to the owners and the confines of the property. Whereas other people were satisfied with a place to work, young James sought a world devoid of confinement, that was limitless and free, without boundaries or fences, figuratively and literally.

As an ambitious young man, James did a few things that would ensure that he lived a grand life and that are worthy of emulation. He sought the mentorship of men who lived beyond the mediocrity that he saw in his family and peers (we often view mediocrity as what we know, what surrounds us, when it actually isn't).

The owner of Airyholme, Thomas Skottowe, recognized the young man's intelligence and paid for him to attend school. He left school early and headed to the seaside village of Staithes, in North Yorkshire, where he apprenticed informally under Skottowe's brother-in-law. He stacked shelves and sliced cheese and bacon, but the proximity to the ocean stirred his soul. At night, Cook would crawl under the shop counter where he slept and study religiously by candlelight all things related to the sea. He avoided grammar and literature and focused solely on mathematics, geography, and astronomy.

**Throughout history, few men have become masters at anything because they had knowledge of everything.** By focusing his studies only on what he was passionate about, only on what would yield success in his field of interest, Cook expedited his acquisition of knowledge in the field.

Too many of us aim to know a little of everything. We like having things to talk about at parties. We like tidbits of information to appear intelligent. That isn't to say you shouldn't acquire a breadth of knowledge and read different kinds of books, but where your passion is concerned, have the discipline to focus your studies intensely on the area to bring yourself closer to your ideal. When it comes to success, a breadth of knowledge isn't pertinent. Napoleon studied battle. Ford studied business. Rockefeller studied trends and money and business. Men who excel delve deeply into what interests them.

Our school system doesn't allow for this. We're taught a little bit about a lot. And we take this approach into other areas of life and wonder why we're not dominating. If there's an aspect of your business that you don't need or feel inclined to master, hire someone who has mastered it. Your focus should be clear.

As Martin Dugard notes in his wonderful book, *Farther Than Any Man*, "Though there would always be detractors in Cook's life—**those who were outraged that a man would dare rise above his preordained rank in Britain's strict class society** —Cook never lost sight of his lofty goals." Cook held a strong belief in himself that complemented his work ethic and courage to venture to new places in pursuit of adventures, glory, and greatness.

He would eventually find work on as a sailor on a mercantile ship, at age 17. He was starting late; the average age of a sailor was 27. To voluntarily seek such work, moreover, was odd. Conditions were awful, and most men were forced into service and many died at sea. Drinking as if each day would be their last was common. It was a hard way to making a living.

Cook persevered and rose through the ranks to command his own ship. This was a lucrative position. Cook, however, didn't want to be confined to the established trade routes of mercantile ships. He boldly turned his back on the money and joined the king's navy, starting again at the bottom, scrubbing decks.

The confidence Cook displayed with such a move is incredible. Throughout his life, he would demonstrate a unique clarity in knowing what he wanted versus what he should want by society's standards. He did not 'stay in his place'. Cook worked harder, studied more, and dared mightier than any of his peers and eventually gained command of a Royal Navy vessel. He would go on to become a world-leading cartographer.

In Cook's time, your place in society was preordained. There was little to no upward mobility between the classes. His drive and daring saw him succeed where others failed and tread where none had tread before. On two occasions in his career he rose, of his own volition, from the bottom to attain the rank of commander, in the mercantile marine and then the Royal Navy.

Cook benefited from no birthright. Nothing about his life was predestined. At birth, his prospects looked bleak. Discipline enabled him to surpass all in his country whose birthright and social standing granted them a ship's command by default, with nothing more than a request.

This is where the notion of the birth lottery should stop, with the proof that success earned does more for a man than success given. The skills and abilities that Cook learned and the passion with which he studied were largely unfamiliar to men assured of rank and command from birth. Birthright provided no incentive for these men to develop the skills to further their craft and them-selves in it or especially to cultivate the traits of grit and discipline that ensured Cook's transcendence of them all. They might excel for a time on the coattails of birthright, but it's the man who strives for and earns success by being better than his competition who equips himself to thrive over time.

A birthright, therefore, does not appear to be a blessing. It doesn't aid in developing you personally or professionally. This is vitally important to admit and to understand. You have to ask the questions:

**Do you want the title, the money, and the fame that comes from holding a certain position or place in society regardless of how you get there? Or do you want the abilities, the skills, the virtues that are won in the process of true achievement?**

By being born with less, you make it far more likely to be able to develop the skills and virtues that achievement will demand you develop because there's no other option. You will not gain success without discipline. Thus, if you really want success, you'll have to become the man that is worthy of it. There is no other way for you, and this has to be seen as a wonderful truth, a grand challenge, not as a curse that so many see it as.

We're told and trained to see ourselves as victims if we start with less, but this cannot be further from the truth. The greatest gift you can be given is having to develop the virtues that greatness requires.

Your stature in society, how you're viewed by your government, or how much money you're born into mean nothing. If you're good at what you do, if you're better than everyone else, someone will want your services and will pay for them.

No matter how low your situation is at birth, it should be seen as a blessing. It doesn't matter if you're a poor farm boy in a time where status is preordained or if you're an indentured servant in Pennsylvania during the 1800s, as was the case for Stephen Smith.

Smith was an indentured servant to a wealthy businessman named Thomas Boude. Boude put Smith to work in his lumber yards along the Columbia waterfront. Smith was essentially a slave, working to one day buy his freedom and start a new life. His position in society was the lowest of the low, hardly something to aspire to, but his abilities, his work ethic, and his attention to detail surpassed those of other men whose social status was above his. So Boude entrusted him with the management of his lumber business. Again, if you're good at what you do someone will notice.

Business owners want to succeed. To do so, they need the best people working for them. Personal politics will eventually lose out to the desire for profits. It doesn't matter if your competition is the CEO's nephew, at some point the cream that rises and is best suited for the job will get an opportunity. If the job isn't given to the best employee, the company will fail, and you'll find another opportunity, unless of course you quit because of a single setback or many, then success will always remain a dream and nothing more.

Smith didn't waste his chance. At the age of 21, he borrowed $50 and bought his release from indenture. But he continued working in Boude's lumberyards as a free man until, in 1822, he went into business for himself. His businesses thrived. In a period where success was often regulated by the color of your skin in many countries, Smith became a millionaire by today's standards.

This slave-turned-success-story isn't singular. From even the worst circumstances disciplined humans are able to succeed, and succeed in a far greater fashion than those who appear to have had a head start in life.

Epictetus, the slave-turned-Stoic philosopher, has a similarly incredible story. He was born into slavery but eventually secured his freedom. Before he became a free man, he studied philosophy. Once he was free, he taught stoicism for 25 years until the Emperor Domitian banished all philosophers from Rome, after which Epictetus fled to Greece and continued teaching until his death.

We still study Epictetus's teachings through the notes taken by one of his students. His legacy has lasted over 2,000 years and will likely continue for 2,000 more, and the man was born a slave.

The point is that this notion of a birth lottery, of nepotism, of society being exclusively built by and for the rich is false. Throughout history, men born into slavery and facing impossible odds still rose to success largely because they disciplined themselves to earn it. More than that, it's almost never been more possible to succeed, though as we continue to grow our governments and the power they have over our lives that will diminish, we still have a far greater opportunity to rise than did the likes of Smith, Epictetus, Cook, and Bonaparte.

It really is a matter of perception.

My peers who've achieved the most success see opportunity, those encumbered by mediocrity or constant failure (which, of course can also be a matter of perspective) see the odds, the obstacles, the futility in effort.

When you see opportunity you believe there is reason to work. When you feel pity for your plight and for the prospects for your future, you will not work, or you will not work *hard enough* and endure *long enough* to see the victory you *need*.

By not believing in opportunity and instead believing in a lack of it, you hurt not only yourself, but your family and friends and the rest of society that would have benefitted from your disciplined effort. Alas, we usually only *feel* pain when it's personal, so think about the life you could possibly have if your dreams were reality. Think about how your family would feel, how proud and free you would feel, if you accomplished what you *really* deep down want to achieve. Now, take that all away from them and yourself. Take it away and replace that successful self with a bitter self, a guy who pity's his life, who hates his work, who is miserable and miserable to be around.

Choose how you view opportunities and obstacles so that this view aligns with the life you want rather than with the life you want to avoid living.

# CHAPTER 3
# The Lost Art
# of Clarity

*When people will not weed their own minds,*
*they are apt to be overrun by nettles.*

—*Horace Walpole*

I was four years old at the time, my family lived in a townhouse in Vancouver, British Columbia. It was a sort of a family housing complex, so everyone had kids. Kids were everywhere of all ages. I had one friend who was a good 3 years older than I was. I think his family was from Hungary. He was a good kid. He had a way with the truth, though.

One time his mom was talking to my old man and she thanked him for his service or something like that. My dad didn't serve in the military, but her son had told her that he was a special operations fella or a CIA type. Anyway, my dad had a good laugh.

Every now and then this kid would bully me, push me around a bit. He was a lot bigger than I was simply because at that age, 3 years is almost 50% more time to spend growing. He was probably a heck of a lot stronger than I was, too. This bullying was something new to me, my first encounter with it, so I didn't know what to do. Even at that time everyone was talking about being peaceful and kind and teaching kids that violence was bad and there wasn't much talk of honor, truth, standing up for yourself, and how to be a man, although - and I'm so thankful my parents did this - I'd grown up having my parents read the Picture Bible to me. My favorite stories were, obviously, of Samson and David, both guys were warriors, killers, defenders and fighters, so I had *always* loved the idea of standing up for what's right, I just didn't really understand what was acceptable and was was not and all of this talk of talking your problems out and how horrible violence was confused the heck out of me. If someone's being violent to you it seemed only logical that fire be fought with fire to earn some semblance of respect.

I went to my old man and told him about the older fella picking on me. My dad sat me down, talked to me about Samson and David and that it's okay to stand up for yourself, in fact, it's GOOD to do so.

That's a *powerful* lesson that fathers have to teach their boys, to stop that first bullying incident with violence, if they don't, they can spend their entire lives living as victims and never truly break free from that mindset. Thank *God* my dad had that conversation with me. It helped shape who I was, how I dealt with future instances, and who I've grown up to be. Had my dad not been around I'm sure my mom would've had a similar conversation with me, but it was different coming from this guy who I thought could kick anyone's ass back then.

The thing he *didn't* tell me was *when* to stand up for myself.

Every couple of days I'd be playing with this kid in our shared backyard. He wouldn't always push me around. In fact, it was in the minority of times that he would. Most of the time we'd just be boys having fun, roughhousing and so forth, getting into trouble. When my dad told me to stand up for myself, I just figured I'd do it the next time I saw the kid, regardless of whether or not he was actually picking on me.

So, from the shared backyard on what must have been a weekend because my dad was home and not at work, I stood there with my buddy who didn't have a clue what was coming. I called out to my old man, *Dad, Dad! Watch this!* My dad, who was in the washroom, stuck his head out the window to witness his son grab the bigger boy from the scruff of his neck and punch the crap out of him. I think I landed a few shots to the gut and the kid went running home crying, again, completely unaware of the attack that was coming his way.

From the john, my dad, with his head out the window, yelled out '*No!*' and ran downstairs. He obviously had to explain *when* it was okay to stand up for myself. You don't do it randomly, you do it when it's the necessary course of action.

Regardless of the surprise attack, my buddy became an even better buddy. He never picked on me again. We had a stronger friendship, one that now contained mutual respect.

Clarity is important.

We can work hard and have discipline, but if it's the wrong kind of discipline or we're walking down the wrong pall, it's all for naught. In that sense, clarity *is* discipline. It's the discipline to determine the correct course of action, to follow the proper thought patterns, to choose to see things in the best possible way for yourself and for the life you want to lead. Without clarity, discipline is useless.

I called this book *The Lost Art of Discipline* because discipline and the clarity needed to achieve it have become far more difficult with the rise of social media *if* you use social media like an increasing number of people choose to use it, as a connection of who they are, as how they measure themselves, as their primary form of communication and entertainment.

Increasingly, we're pushed to base our value not on a personally defined path but in comparison with how people portray themselves in their feeds or profiles or pages. That's not really how life works, and it takes discipline to be able to separate what we're told from what's real.

Whatever path you choose, don't compete on the basis of hollow value. Instead, win.

We can each have our definitions of winning, which can change over time and with compounding experiences. Being that we can define victory in whichever way we want so long as it includes achievement in some form or another, and everything that achievement requires of us (persistence, grit, hard work, discipline), we *need* victory to live a good life.

Winning can be living an adventurous life. It may mean becoming wealthy or owning a lot of land or spending the vast majority of time doing things you love to do and very little time doing things you don't love to do. Winning can mean raising a family and being the leader of your own tribe.

However you define victory, winning must fulfill you, and it has to be a challenge to achieve it. The greater the challenge, I believe, the better, because it'll bring that much more out of you, it'll teach you more. If you define victory by someone else's standard, you'll win their game, which won't give you the fulfillment you crave.

Accomplishment is a necessary aspect of our time here. If, however, we accomplish the wrong things, we're not going to get the joy, the pride, or the sense of purpose that we should gain from victory.

For years, I had the wrong idea of what victory was. And it makes sense—I was a young punk kid who wanted to be better than everyone else. I wanted more money, more power, greater stature.

**My idea of victory stemmed not from the truth, the core of who I wanted to become and what I wanted to do, but from insecurity.**

Be wary of this. Be cognizant of why you're aiming to achieve what you want to achieve. I wanted to be better than people. I wanted to have money *purely* because I didn't grow up with it but I grew up around it. I still want money, probably a lot more than I used to want, it's just something that motivates me. But I want it now because of the freedom it can provide and the good it can help me do and the power it gives an individual over his life, his family's, his future. I want it because it's a form of measurement. It, like a lot of other metrics, can tell me how good I am at what I do.

To be honest the main reason is power. I've seen how life throws unexpected tragedy into the laps of everyone, and how being financially powerful and free can, at the very least, help solve or help some of these unexpected tragedies or bumps in the road for myself, but even more-so for my family and friends. That's power in my eyes, to be able to solve problems on a big scale for some people, without even having to think about it because the resources to do so are there, and are plenty.

Knowing why you pursue what you pursue adds real meaning to the pursuit. It helps you stay focused. It helps you stay motivated. It helps you determine what projects to do, which ones are in line with your values, and which you should avoid. When it's purely about money, you'll do anything to make money. When it's about creating a legacy, about doing good work that you can be proud of that's a part of that legacy, you're more discerning about what projects to take on and you stay true to your values, which ends up being a very powerful thing down the road.

Before you define victory, know that it must include the following if it is to be true, if it is to deliver what you want it to deliver:

**Purpose, Meaning, Accomplishment, and,
least importantly, Happiness.**

We're a society obsessed with happiness. It's a destructive primary pursuit because it's a mood, an emotion. We can choose to be happy amid pain and anguish, but most often we choose to be sad and angry in a situation that really doesn't require us to feel that way.

Lacking happiness is, by and large, a choice. You can change this by focusing on gratitude and on the good in your life, and a challenge can be a good thing if you see it as an opportunity to improve rather than a curse. If, however, you lack meaning, purpose, and accomplishment, you will have a life devoid of validity and will not feel as if you're living a good life.

Purpose, meaning, and accomplishment are choices, just like happiness, but they have a result. They force you to act every day in accordance with whatever you're pursuing or becoming.

Victory needs each of the first three. It's merely nice if you have the fourth.

## The Dream

*I dream my painting and I paint my dream.*

—*Vincent Van Gogh*

Success stories begin with vision and are carried out by disciplined habits.

Before you can paint a picture of what you've created, of the life you've built for yourself and your family, you must dream the picture. Without a direction, a clear pursuit and goal, we wander. Man is not supposed to wander.

**Write the picture of your perfect day as if you had to live this same day, every day, for the remainder of your life.**

Make your ideal true, and personal.

Be honest about what you want in life and who you want to become. Don't sell yourself short. Don't think that someone else's vision has to be yours, but by all means use models of the past or present to construct your ideal. To live like Theodore Roosevelt did, filled with action and adventure, is admirable and something every man should look to.

Be specific. Write about the sights, smells, and sounds as you wake up; about the time you wake up; and about who you wake up next to. Write about your ideal clients, the people you're helping and working with. Make note of everything. Write about how productive you are and how you ward off distraction.

Be clear about why you're working, who you're working for, and why you've created this idyllic day for yourself and your family.

This perfect day—your perfect wake-up time, energy level, focus for your work, evening, time with your family—is an incredibly important exercise. We're going to bring it home in a few steps, but defining your dream, not just a goal for work or a house you want to buy, but your dream, gives you a framework for bringing your dream into your present reality.

Much of what you write does not have to involve only future aspirations. But it is important that you write as audaciously as your imagination allows while remaining honest about what you write.

Write the story that is your ideal day here on earth with work and family included.

Now, how are you going to build this?

My ideal business is based on this Benjamin Franklin quote:

> *"If you wou'd not be forgotten*
> *As soon as you are dead and rotten,*
> *Either write things worth reading,*
> *or do things worth the writing."*

The "write things worth reading" thought from Franklin is broad, but simple. It fits with my line of work. If I write things worth reading then that's work well done.

This book, and the Man Diet, is the start. Hopefully, it gives some value to some people or a lot of value to a lot of people.

Franklin's advice to "do things worth the writing" is powerful. To live a life worthy of being made into a movie, I think, is the ideal. To embark on adventures too ambitious for the minds of most people to even entertain and somehow make it a business is the dream.

When we understand our aim, we can figure out what habits we'll need to develop to inch closer to that ideal every day of our lives. Knowing that writing is a part of my ideal business, be it a publishing company or writing books people enjoy, means that I have to read and write every day without exception.

So what's your ideal business?

What kind of company do you want to run or what kind of position do you want to have within that company?

What kind of work do you want to do? What kind of worker do you want to be?

Keep in mind that the life you envision for yourself has to coexist with this business or your place in the company you work for. I love to hustle and to work; it's a large part of why I'm here, why we're all here. We're not here to party. We're not here for pleasure. We are here to suffer, and suffering takes many forms. It's in suffering that we grow, evolve, appreciate, and love, truly love. Pleasure, though it has its time and place, is often a band-aid, it covers up the truth.

An important question to ask is, what do you want to create?

Is it a movement? Is it a collection of books? Is it an online empire? Do you literally want to build buildings, houses, neighborhoods? Do you want to create a legacy? What form does that legacy take?

Another important question is, what do you want to solve?

**Or, do you want to use what you earn to grow wealth through investments, through managing your money well and watching it compound over time?**

Ideally you'll take what you're learning in your job and start your own business. It gives you much more control over your time, how much you earn, and how much you fork over to the government in taxes.

Many people who live their ideal lives don't place importance on their work. Their work provides the means to live the life they want to live. I know a few guys who have this outlook, and they are damn motivated to do their best at their career, but only because of who they provide for and who they're actually working for (their family). Whatever you want with your work, you have to aim high and to be the best you can be. There's no point going through the motions when all that success takes is a little more clarity, discipline, and hard work.

When you have your ideal life in mind, bring it to a more tangible state by putting it on paper.

### What Will You Be?

*First say to yourself what you would be;*
*and then do what you have to do.*

—*Epictetus*

A decade ago, I was introduced to Stoicism as a result of watching one of my favorite movies, *Gladiator*. The film is fiction, but it has historical figures woven into its story. One of them is the Roman emperor Marcus Aurelius. I was curious to know if he had actually lived, so I looked him up.

I soon after bought *Meditations*, a collection of thoughts and letters by Marcus Aurelius, a walking, breathing oxymoron of an emperor who, despite access to anything he wanted, practiced a philosophy of discipline, minimalism, temperance, and frugality. Reading this man's thoughts, I recalled a thought that I'd either heard or read whose logic stated that it is not impressive to be peaceful if you do not possess the capacity to be dangerous.

In the same sense, it would not be admirable to be frugal if that was your only option. But here was an emperor who shunned the opulence of his position, and I found this incredibly intriguing.

The letters he wrote to himself and that he never intended for publication for posterity provide almost every sound piece of advice you need to live a good, purposeful, flourishing life.

Marcus Aurelius led me to the teachings of Epictetus, which are actually collections of notes taken by a student of his because he, too, never sat down to document his thoughts or philosophies with the intention of having them published. Epictetus, a former slave, practiced the same philosophy of Stoicism as Marcus Aurelius, a Roman emperor.

It is a philosophy that, in my mind, is about power (I may be alone in this perspective on Stoicism, but hear me out). The individual exercises power in choosing how to react to an event rather than permitting an event to determine how he reacts, thinks, and lives. It teaches you to understand what you can and can't control, which is a big part of what discipline is, and how we can be truly happy no matter our circumstances. You should not even *attempt* to dwell on or control what you have no control over, like a tragedy or an event. You *should*, however, exact entire control over what you do have control over, like how you react to the event, which thoughts you choose to follow, and what you do with your time.

Epictetus laid it out like this:

*"In life our first job is this, to divide and distinguish things into two categories: externals I cannot control, but the choices I make with regard to them I do control. Where will I find good and bad? In me, in my choices."*

Discipline is understanding and acting on only the things that are within your control. It's using the power you have to make whatever decision you want to make in the battle of what you want now versus what you want most. It's using the power you have to choose how you think, how you see the world and the work that you do, and what mood you choose to be in.

Stoicism is about finding opportunity in tragedy and pain and creating what you want even if the prospects initially look less than promising.

Never before in human history has it been more crucial to adopt the ancient philosophy of Stoicism. It has influenced many historical figures, and modern men should take heed.

Theodore Roosevelt kept Aurelius's *Meditations* and Epictetus's *Enchiridion* close as he navigated the perils of the Amazon River after his presidency. George Washington's introduction to the Stoics at age seventeen influenced his habits and thoughts. Economist Adam Smith studied Marcus Aurelius as a youth. Thomas Jefferson died with a copy of Seneca's writings on his nightstand.

In college, I took a philosophy course that completely ruined my desire to read any further philosophy. There was no truth, just opinion. There was no action, just thought. The teacher was a lost, weak soul who couldn't make it in the real world, so he decided to mold young minds in the education system. He didn't understand life. He was opinionated and entitled. He wasn't concerned with living well but telling others how to live. He was the exact opposite of who I wanted to become, and yet, he was charged with moulding minds and showing young people how to form opinions about life.

Thank God for *Gladiator*! It opened my eyes to the teachings and actions of Marcus Aurelius, Cato, Seneca, and Epictetus and, more, to the guidelines that helped them and other men conquer their fears and overcome all obstacles en route, in the case of some men, to conquering the then known world.

The Stoics are kings of discipline and of knowing what does and what does not deserve time, energy, and thought. It's a philosophy especially applicable to today's rampant consumerism. We have become slaves to buying in the moment because we falsely believe that possessions dictate our value and that the illusion of the momentary joy that we get from a purchase is real happiness.

We live in a dangerous society where comparison is preeminent. We judge ourselves based not on our deeds but compared with what our neighbor has accomplished or purchased. Stoicism forces you to **stay in your lane**, which is the only place you should be aiming to live. You have too much to work on. Your goals and dreams are far too important, you cannot give your time and energy to focusing on what someone else is doing, has done, or has.

## Aim to Be Better

*To feel ambition and to act upon it is to embrace the unique calling of our souls. Not to act upon that ambition is to turn our backs on ourselves and on the reason for our existence.*

—*Steven Pressfield*

Humans are not born perfect. Actually, we're born rather useless and dependent. This move to tell kids that they're perfect just the way they are is a horrible one, and something that robs the individual of the desire to improve, which is a necessity in life. We need to be better tomorrow than we are today. That's a constant throughout life.

Our culture tells us to look and act a certain part, but it fails to push us to play the part that will get us paid and provide us value and help us win. You need to be great at something, anything, if you're going win, whether that greatness is parenthood or being an honorable man or being a leader, a teacher, a server of others.

A valuable thing you gain from studying the Stoics is the ability to decipher what is and is not true. Stoicism shows you which desires are genuine for your mission in life and which desires merely fill a void in the present. **The fundamental of discipline is choosing between what you want now and what you want most.**

To address this issue—and it should be addressed in every decision-making situation—you have to know who you are. You are not lost. You do not need to find yourself. Sure, you're creating yourself, daily actually, but you are not wandering lost on this planet that's lost in this universe. You have purpose and direction.

Who you are is determined every day by your habits, your thoughts, your opinions, your worldview. As such, you will not rise to the occasion by chance; you will rely on your training to deal with any circumstance.

You are not a winner if you think you're a winner. Your habits and daily actions need to reflect the actions of a winner regardless of whether or not victory has arrived. How simple and powerful is that? All you have to do is change your habits and you become who you want to become, the man who daily brings victory closer to the present. If you don't, you'll be the man who daily pushes victory further into the future.

Are you training to become a better man and a better person? Or are you fixated on the wrong things? To know the answer to those questions, you have to know who you are: what you stand for, live for, and would die for.

- What are your values?

- What are the virtues that you won't compromise no matter how the public is behaving or which way the masses are trending?

- Who is the man you're trying to become, how does he act, how does he think, how does he carry himself?

Answer those questions. Take out a notepad and write them down. Ponder them next time you're hiking. Craft your ideals, your standards as a guide to keep you pointed in the direction you most want to go and not in the direction of what you want in the moment.

If you want to be a guy who gets more work done in less time, who doesn't get distracted, who does good work that's valuable to others, that's who you can become. You can become the guy who's in impeccable shape. You can become the shoulder that others lean on because you show courage in the face of tragedy. You can become the leader that you always looked up to growing up but never quite became.

Think about archetypes you know or have read about or seen on the silver screen. Just because a character is fictional doesn't mean it's charisma can't be developed in reality. Take Theodore Roosevelt's energy, John D. Rockefeller's meticulousness and consistency, Robert E. Lee's sense of honor, Marcus Aurelius's discipline, and James Bond's confidence.

Reread the quote from Epictetus about our first job. When you find your models, defining how you think and what you can control becomes easier because you hold yourself to their ideal and not the one you've slid into over time after years of being told you're an average, normal, run-of-the-mill fella who's going to amount to little.

Your ideal life begins with a vision. Then you must realize it through action and right thinking.

**You cannot live a grand life if you're constantly focusing, worrying about, and whining about things that are out of your control. Leave them be. Focus on what you can control, and focus on that alone.**

## The Process

*The gods had condemned Sisyphus to ceaselessly rolling a rock to the top of a mountain, whence the stone would fall back of its own weight. They had thought with some reason that there is no more dreadful punishment than futile and hopeless labor.*

That's what it feels like if you're working for an end, a goal, a dream. We feel as though we're toiling without accomplishment.

It's the wrong outlook.

The focus cannot be the end but the process. It's the struggle, the pushing of the stone that strengthens your body and your mind; it's almost irrelevant where you are on the mountain. Forget about the summit, there is no summit, just the climb.

*You just laid out your vision. Now come to grips with the fact that the vision is simply where you've pointed yourself. It's the direction in which you've decided to head. The process, the means by which you'll get there, is everything.*

Life is the struggle and the pain. It's who you are every day, not what you're awarded or rewarded with. Those things are nice, and they'll come, but they'll come as a result of the struggle and the pain.

I hate to call this a self-help book, but it is. I hate to call it that because a lot of self-help books—at least many that I've read—are weightless. They're made up of theory and much hollow talk. They make promises that end up taking away the self-reliance that the term self-help implies. They leave in their wake dreamers and wishers and envious people who want to avoid the pain and struggle that every day life has consisted of throughout mankind's history.

Keep your vision in mind for clarity's sake, but don't spend too much time in the future because it can lead to wishing, and wishing is cancerous, it eats away at you, making you hate where you are and what you have to do to get to where you want to go.

Over the past few months I've found myself in this state of being incredibly unhappy with where I am because I'm comparing it to where I want to be and even where some very successful friends are. What brought me back to the present was talking with older, more successful entrepreneurs who saw my business, the revenues, the lack of headaches or potential headaches because of the lightweight nature of my business, and looked at *it* and my position and my age with a hint of envy. It's all perspective. Decide where you want to go, choose the vehicle that will get you there, and then become the best driver of that vehicle on the planet.

The only competitive advantage that can consistently be replicated isn't talent or help, but actively learning more than your competition. Stay in your lane. Stay in the moment. And hustle.

## Your Mission

*A mission statement is not something you write overnight... But fundamentally, your mission statement becomes your constitution, the solid expression of your vision and values. It becomes the criterion by which you measure everything else in your life.*

*—Stephen Covey*

Your mission is an expression of who you are, your vision, your values. It is not a pipe dream or a wish. It isn't an attempt to create an image, to show others a side of yourself that you want them to see or to convey success without actually having it.

Your mission is the strongest, toughest, most accomplished version of yourself that you put forth every single day.

It starts as a goal, but it becomes a way of life.

Actually, it's more than a way of life. A way of life sounds monotonous. There's nothing exciting or challenging about a way of life. As Covey puts it, "It becomes the criterion by which you measure everything else in your life." It's everything. It's why you're here, what you're here to do, how you're here to be remembered.

It's the reason you form certain habits and drop others. It's an energy-giver, the sheer scope of what you're trying to do, the mission you're on, scares you a little. It gives you an energy source that's far more powerful than any oral stimulant. You've created (not found) your challenge, and now your days are spent moving closer to its fulfillment.

A mission is a powerful thing.

It isn't as trivial as a goal. It's not a benchmark. It isn't a milestone. A mission is something that encompasses you, it becomes infinitely more important than anything else, and everything else then aligns to move you closer to your mission.

If you have ambition - and you do, because this book is useless to a human without ambition - you do not merely act in a manner that will bring you a little closer to a watered-down version of your mission. Why aim at anything if you're not going to aim at the top, the best, the most elite point you can possibly aim at?

Your mission takes over your life, if it's truly a mission, and you begin to *live* the success you aspire to create. You rise earlier, you stay focused on a single task for a longer period of time, you invest your earnings back into your business and you live lean, you train, you study relentlessly, spending your waking moments learning more than your competition - which is a sustainable competitive advantage rarely spoken of.

Your releases and escapes feed your clarity. You hunt, explore, hike. Everything in your life is a manifestation of your mission. You become your ideal, down to your thoughts, your expressions, your ideas and ambitions. The ebbs and flows of life, they do not deter your actions, they do not sully your intentions. Your feelings don't get in the way of your work.

You *are* successful even before you've become successful. You become the ideal that will fulfill the mission. You train to improve, grow, and gain, and then you simply *are*.

Your mission isn't a weightless goal that you write in your diary. It's an expression of who you optimally are, who you're here to become, and why you're here on this damn planet. Don't, then, write whispers. Don't allow the limited thinking of your upbringing bring reality into your equation. Don't set your sights on the safety and security of the goals of those around you, of those you know, of aims you know you can achieve.

Your mission isn't your passion. In our society of 'follow your passion' and 'you're great' even though you've never accomplished anything, you do not set out to play in the NBA if you suck at basketball and you have no intention of practicing 12 hours a day. Anthony Bourdain put it wonderfully, "It's not always a great idea to 'follow your passion.' If you're passionate about something you will NEVER be good at, at some point, you're gonna have to recognize that. But if you feel in your heart, if you know, if you have reason to believe that you could be awesome at something—that you can do something unique that will shock and astound and terrify and bewitch them—do that."

Passion and mission often *don't* align. Of the friends of mine that are successful and on their way to being *very* successful, none of them followed their passion, but each of them sought and took advantage of the opportunity that was in front of them, and continue to grab ahold of opportunities that cross their paths that are often disguised under hard work and labor.

They took advantage of mentors, of the challenges that opportunities presented, and *created* passion after they found success. At first it was an opportunity and a challenge, but it eventually became rewarding and fruitful.

Mike Rowe, explains his stance on not following your passion in this write up he posted on social media some years ago:

Hi Stephen A few years ago, I did a special called "The Dirty Truth." In it, I challenged the conventional wisdom of popular platitudes by offering "dirtier," more individualistic alternatives. For my inspiration, I looked to those hackneyed bromides that hang on the walls of corporate America. The ones that extoll passersby to live up to their potential by "dreaming bigger," "working smarter," and being a better "team player." In that context, I first saw "Follow Your Passion" displayed in the conference room of a telemarketing firm that employed me thirty years ago. The words appeared next to an image of a rainbow, arcing gently over a waterfall and disappearing into a field of butterflies. Thinking of it now still makes me throw up in my mouth.

Like all bad advice, "Follow Your Passion" is routinely dispensed as though it's wisdom were both incontrovertible and equally applicable to all. It's not. Just because you're passionate about something doesn't mean you won't suck at it. And just because you're determined to improve doesn't mean that you will. Does that mean you shouldn't pursue a thing you're passionate about?" Of course not. The question is, for how long, and to what end?

When it comes to earning a living and being a

productive member of society – I don't think people should limit their options to those vocations they feel passionate towards. I met a lot of people on Dirty Jobs who really loved their work. But very few of them dreamed of having the career they ultimately chose. I remember a very successful septic tank cleaner who told me his secret of success. "I looked around to see where everyone else was headed, and then I went the opposite way," he said. "Then I got good at my work. Then I found a way to love it. Then I got rich."

Every time I watch The Oscars, I cringe when some famous movie star – trophy in hand – starts to deconstruct the secret to happiness. It's always the same thing, and I can never hit "mute" fast enough to escape the inevitable cliches. "Don't give up on your dreams kids, no matter what." "Don't let anyone tell you that you don't have what it takes." And of course, "Always follow your passion!"

Today, we have millions looking for work, and millions of good jobs unfilled because people are simply not passionate about pursuing those particular opportunities. Do we really need Lady GaGa telling our kids that happiness and success can be theirs if only they follow their passion?

There are many examples – including those you mention – of passionate people with big dreams who stayed the course, worked hard, overcame adversity, and changed the world though sheer pluck and determination. We love stories that begin with a dream, and culminate when that dream comes true. And to your question, we would surely be worse off without the likes of Bill Gates and Thomas Edison and all the other innovators and Captains of Industry. But from my perspective, I don't see a shortage of people who are willing to dream big.

I see people struggling because their reach has exceeded their grasp.

I'm fascinated by the beginning of American Idol. Every year, thousands of aspiring pop-stars show up with great expectations, only to learn that they don't have anything close to the skills they thought they did. What's amazing to me, isn't their lack of talent – it's their lack of awareness, and the resulting shock of being rejected. How is it that so many people are so blind to their own limitations? How did these people get the impression they could sing in the first place? Then again, is their incredulity really so different than the surprise of a college graduate who learns on his first interview that his double major in Medieval Studies and French Literature doesn't guarantee him the job he expected? In a world where everyone gets a trophy, encouragement trumps honesty, and realistic expectations go out the window.

When I was 16, I wanted to follow in my grandfathers footsteps. I wanted to be a tradesman. I wanted to build things, and fix things, and make things with my own two hands. This was my passion, and I followed it for years. I took all the shop classes at school, and did all I could to absorb the knowledge and skill that came so easily to my granddad. Unfortunately, the handy gene skipped over me, and I became frustrated. But I remained determined to do whatever it took to become a tradesman.

One day, I brought home a sconce from woodshop that looked like a paramecium, and after a heavy sigh, my grandfather told me the truth. He explained that my life would be a lot more satisfying and productive if I got myself a different kind of toolbox. This was almost certainly the best advice I've ever received, but at the time, it was crushing. It felt contradictory to everything I knew about persistence, and the importance of "staying the course." It felt like quitting. But here's the "dirty truth," Stephen. "Staying the course" only makes sense if you're headed in a sensible direction. Because passion and persistence – while most often associated with success – are also essential ingredients of futility.

That's why I would never advise anyone to "follow their passion" until I understand who they are, what they want, and why they want it. Even then, I'd be cautious. Passion is too important to be without, but too fickle to be guided by. Which is why I'm more inclined to say, "Don't Follow Your Passion, But Always Bring it With You."

Carry On, Mike

Regardless of your mission, you do not create the mission by following only a feeling. Feelings fade. Opportunities lead to other opportunities.

Too many people these days and for the past couple of decades, see their reason for being here in the form of what they like to do, regardless of whether or not what they like to do can support their family, or if they're actually *good* at what they like to do, or if it makes them a productive member of society.

It's all about feeling, and not about truth and reality.

Find the opportunity - we all have them - and start there. Then, *become* the guy who's *great* at what he does, who outperforms his competition, whether or not the reward is yet in sight. Be great before you're great.

**Discipline is choosing what you want most
instead of what you want now.**

We have to set ourselves in a direction. We have to determine what vehicle to take to get there. And then we have to focus on the habits and routines that'll bring us success, that will bring us closer to that ideal, faster.

Your mission may be to acquire wealth and the power that comes with it, the power to help others, the power to stave off crisis, the power to live wherever you want, and the vehicle that gets you there may present itself in an employment opportunity in a field that you're not *passionate* about, per se, but you grow to appreciate, especially when you begin to realise your mission.

If you're not 'following your passion', find the opportunity and become passionate about being great.

# SECTION 2

# HOW TO BECOME
# MORE DISCIPLINED

# CHAPTER 4

# Taking Action

*Do you want to know who you are? Don't ask.*
*Act! Action will delineate and define you.*

—*Thomas Jefferson*

## Review: Four Steps to Your Ideal Day

Being great or effective or becoming the person you want to become is not complicated. We want it to seem complicated, to seem as though it's just out of reach or not quite worth the effort or a puzzle that our wee brains can't quite solve so that we can excuse ourselves from giving our maximal effort.

*It is* simple. All you have to do is:

1. **Define your path**

   Identify the path you want to take in life.

   We need a path, a dream, a focus, a direction. Have you ever been unemployed? The first day or two is kinda fun. We think we have freedom. We can do whatever we want.

After a few days, the lack of direction, purpose, and meaning in our lives is constricting. Forget that no money is coming in, it's the life devoid of direction that's crippling.

Humans are always going in some direction. It's better to create your own direction than aimlessly wander in someone else's.

Define your ideal path, then compound it. Make it bigger, grander, more epic.

Make it daring. Let fear guide you rather than deter you. You know what I'm referring to. It's the dream you've always had, the man you've always wanted to become but you're too afraid to take the leap, to accept the risk that is the time and effort and work that this goal, this dream, this ideal calls for.

Dare mightier.

Every self-help book on the planet will tell you to dream big. But they leave it at that.

Your goals and dreams have to be grand, awesome in the truest sense of the word, if you're going to extract from them what you need: energy.

The mere idea of daring and audacious goals has power within it. Such goals give you unbelievable energy through the excitement of possibly achieving them and the fear of failing. Both sources are equally potent and powerful.

Mediocre, mundane goals don't have that effect. You give to them, but they don't give back.

A daring goal, a path that's worthy of your talents, abilities, and ambition, brings with it an energy that enables adherence. It's what you really want, and that typically multiplies the energy tenfold. The thing about goals is that they're not always easy to set. Oftentimes, you need an outside perspective to help you.

Your goal might be to write a book. So you determine how many words you need to write every day. Perhaps you want to run a marathon or you have five different goals in five different areas of your life, which is ideal. Whatever your goals, they have to be challenging. They have to be bigger than what you think you can actually achieve so that you get the benefit of fear and excitement from what you're undertaking.

Define an ideal, a path, a big goal, something to move toward.

2. **Specify your goals**

When you identify your ideal, how you want to live, who you want to be, then reverse engineer the details to bring it closer to the present.

Discipline is focusing on the process. But without identifying the process, we too often show a lack of discipline by focusing on areas that are insignificant and out of line with our ideal. Set a direction, then determine the habits necessary to go in that direction. If something pulls you off of this defined path, leave it, and instead focus on something that moves you forward toward your desired end.

A good question to ask is, what am I doing now that isn't pushing my business forward?

Quite often the answer will lead you to hire

someone, delegate a task to somebody, or drop something completely. You have to focus on your daily processes if you want to bring this massively audacious goal into something immediate.

**If a goal is allowed to stay in the future, to remain a year, two years, three years ahead, you risk not having the urgency that will help you focus on what really matters: the correct process.**

If a goal remains too far in the future, it makes it difficult to place enough importance on what you do in the present. Specify the things that you need to accomplish within three to six months to bring you closer to your chosen path. Don't go beyond six months, as that time frame lacks the urgency, clarity, and excitement that you need to win.

This book, for my example, is something I've been working on for over a year. When I brought that annual revenue down from a five-year to a six-month goal, I needed to do something big to move the business and my life closer to my dream. I suddenly had to finish the book in three months, which meant hiring an editor, a company to help me format the book, and a graphics guy to help me create the cover. It also meant, of course, setting aside time daily for writing this hopefully delightful read.

When the revenue goal was a pipe dream, a future quest, I didn't need the write the book. I didn't need to stop wasting time on purposeless activities. I didn't need to structure my article writing day or my video filming day; I could leave everything to the muse, to the myth that ideas come when they come and that we can't control if or when they arrive.

Specify your goals and then identify a few things that need to happen for you to attain them.

3.  **Do the right things**

Accomplishment is important.

Yet, we're often doing things in the moment that are taking us further away from what we deem as accomplishment.

You're not going to have a 100 percent success rate right off the bat. The goal is to get better daily. The simplest method I've found is to grab a piece of paper, write out my goal, and then align my tasks during the day to that goal. This review process isn't done monthly or weekly, but daily. Not only to ensure that I'm headed in the right direction, but to maintain that excitement I had when I initially set out on this path.

This book is at the top of the list. Second on the list is generating articles and YouTube videos that will get more eyes onto the site and bring in more leads and customers.

Checking my Facebook page isn't on the list. Reading an article or watching a video isn't found on the list.

You can start with a broad goal, like a revenue goal for your business, but then you have to specify the thing that will make the biggest impact on that broad goal. From there, you have to prioritize the tasks you need to accomplish, starting with the task that will—when accomplished—help you make the biggest leap toward that specific goal and then go from there.

Anything that doesn't move the needle doesn't get added to your list of tasks and therefore doesn't make it into your day.

4. **Schedule**

Create a schedule that will bring you success.

It's simple. We're going to delve deeper into this in the coming chapters, but suffice it to say here that you must block off time for your most important tasks. Wake up earlier. Go to bed earlier. Schedule your workout time.

**Your day is a page in the book of your life. Win a day, win a life. Define the process by which you'll achieve victory daily, and do it every day.**

## Choices

*Regret for the things we did can be*
*tempered by time; it is regret for the things*
*we did not do that is inconsolable.*

*—Sydney J. Harris*

Imagine doing what you're doing right now for the remainder of your life.

You sleep in, you get distracted easily, you don't save or invest your money. You work hard. You do a lot of the right things. But you do just enough of the wrong things that who you want to become forever eludes you.

Who you want to become is who you're required to become to live the life you identify as your ideal. Be careful what you wish for, though. All of the money and power in the world won't bring you the meaning and purpose you want. You need relationships. You need discipline in all areas of your life, not just in business.

Imagine being 88 years old and on your deathbed, realizing that you accomplished none of your most ambitious dreams. Imagine lying there, about to take your final breath, and being filled with the regret of never having lived the adventurous, daring life you thought you would live when you were a kid or a teen dreaming about the man you'd one day become.

The biggest regret is inevitably the regret of inaction. You rationalized not doing something for years, and now, finally, you can't do it even if you want to.

It may seem masochistic, but thinking about the possibility of future regret can be - and should be - a powerful driving force, a reminder the our time here is very limited, and the decision to avoid doing things because of fear or laziness not only makes absolutely no sense when we look at our lives in their totality, but can be incredibly destructive as well.

**Imagine never having lived a disciplined life.**

You didn't spend enough time with your family, which is a huge regret. You never broke off and did your own thing. You spent your entire life worrying about finances because you lacked focus and discipline in how you allocated what you earned. You earned enough to save and build wealth, but your desires left you always walking the line between being broke and barely surviving.

Be in that regret. Feel that pain. Exist there for a moment.

Go deeper. See your son's face, look in his eyes and imagine not being a part of his life because you were too busy being too busy (rarely a sign of being efficient and effective).

Think about the things in life that excite you. Maybe it's a bucket list. They can be done, they can be won, along with the work you *must* get done. The two dreams, the multiple wishes, do not oppose one another so long as you have discipline.

**Discipline is doing what you set out to do.**

Everyone can and does dream. They wish without working. They talk about what they want to do, and they leave it at words or wishes and never develop the discipline to do the work.

What's incredibly powerful is the fact that we learn by doing, not by listening or being taught. We solve problems, find solutions, and discover what we need to know to gain what we want to gain through *doing*, not wishing or preparing to do, but diving in head first and learning in the real world, with skin in the game, not as an observer, or as Theodore Roosevelt would say, *a critic*. You'll read this quote again, but it's important to put here.

*"It is not the critic who counts; not the man who points out how the strong man stumbles, or where the doer of deeds could have done them better. The credit belongs to the man who is actually in the arena, whose face is marred by dust and sweat and blood; who strives valiantly; who errs, who comes short again and again, because there is no effort without error and shortcoming; but who does actually strive to do the deeds; who knows great enthusiasms, the great devotions; who spends himself in a worthy cause; who at the best knows in the end the triumph of high achievement, and who at the worst, if he fails, at least fails while daring greatly, so that his place shall never be with those cold and timid souls who neither know victory nor defeat."*

Discipline is adding action to your most ambitious dreams. It's giving life to what your soul, your innermost being, is begging you to do. It needs you to develop discipline so you can carry out the life you're destined to live, that you need to live if you're going to be able to live your final days with the pride of having lived a great and good and meaningful life and not with regret.

This is your one life. That doesn't mean you're the most important person on the planet or that you're entitled to anything. It does mean that your choices have consequences, and ones that are final. You do not get another go at this thing. Stop waiting for a helping hand or for someone to come along to show you the way or to give you the push you need to become the man you need to become, to take the massive action you need to take.

You're dying. Your decisions matter. Dreams are just wishes if they don't have discipline. Make the right decisions. Then act on those decisions.

Furthermore, do not prepare for too long. Do. Preparation can be the excuse that you lean on preventing you from action, from having to take the leap, incur the risk that investment both monetary and in time demand you to take on to achieve.

# CHAPTER 5

# Moving from Vision to Action

*The choice is discipline or regret. The options are not all that abundant.*

When you have your north star, the direction you want to head, the focus becomes only the steps you must take to move in that direction. This is imperative if you're to develop the discipline that success demands you develop. Everything else doesn't exist in a moment where you're focusing on one of those steps, and it's these steps that must rule your life and your decision-making process.

Focusing on the process allows us to attend to only what matters, the work that must be done, and not get lost in this often depressing idea of how far we are from where we'd like to be.

While there's a lot I need to complete, as I'm sure you do as well, there can only be one *most* important task. Thus, the first half of my day is given to this book. The second half of the day is given to filming and other writing and so on. This will continue until the book is done. And then a new most important task will take its place.

This way, more things get done at a higher quality in less time. There's congruence and momentum in my day, week, and month.

What's more is that the book takes as long or as little as it needs to take to be completed. There isn't a day where I have set aside to have it completed by. It's a book, not an appointment.

My previous book was finished far earlier than I thought it would be. This one's taking longer.

Without clarity about where you're headed and what you need to do to get there, and the acceptance that only one thing can be done in a moment, that divided attention is as useless as a glass hammer, you will not accomplish your goals, nor will you have the peace that comes from the process.

**Clarity is as important as hard work and persistence.**

Thinking is as important as doing. Though, when you're doing you cannot be doing other things as well because you rob yourself of two powerful states: deep work, and flow.

Deep work and flow are being completely involved in what you're doing, which would seem to be the only way in which one *would work*, but at least in my life, I've spent more time out of this state than it in when it comes to both life, work, and hobbies. The futility of focusing on more than one thing at a time is obvious, it doesn't work. Yet, especially today, we've made divided attention the norm, and focused, singular attention a rarity.

I *understood* that focusing on a single thing is not only more effective, as it gives you less stress and worry while allowing you to live to a higher standard, but I couldn't - or wouldn't, rather - put this knowledge into practice.

As you may know, I have an online business. I write articles and create programs that help guys - and sometimes girls - get in better shape or get better work done or develop the virtues that will help them create the lives they want by becoming the men they need to become to achieve their aspirations. The internet is a series of time-wasting opportunities. Social media is a large part of my business - one I'm turning my back on a lot more these days - so checking how a post is doing or how other entrepreneurs are marketing their brand or business can derail a possibly productive work day. Doing research on a program or topic can lead to reading that has nothing to do with the initial focus of the research.

Divided attention can, if you're not careful, become almost habitual and routine. After a while of working online I automatically checked my phone frequently to see earnings or how a post did. I *began* my day by checking and responding to emails. I answered messages on my Facebook account before I even *began to work*.

After slipping into this way of 'working' I found myself unhappy with what I was doing, incredibly unfulfilled with my work, and insanely stressed every single day. I was mastering the *new* art of being busy while turning my back on the *lost art* of being disciplined.

I felt like I was working hard, but again, I was hardly working. We can *feel* like we're working hard, but feelings are so often lies. We can feel like we're not fulfilled, but in truth, we're simply not focused enough and disciplined enough. We *would be fulfilled* if we were getting more work completed, and if our business was doing better than it currently is, or if we were improving daily and learning daily. We can *feel* worried about our future, but that feeling would be squashed if we'd only get better and a greater amount of work done in the present.

I can still feel the 100-pound dumbbell that felt like it was constantly resting on my chest, or the boa constrictor that seemed to be constricting my breathing. I was stressed beyond stressed. I was constantly worried, perpetually jumping from task-to-task without anything real to show for it. Business began to slip, revenue dipped and expenses rose, and I could have *sworn* that I was working harder than ever, but was I?

What's 'work'?

Is trying to do a bunch of things at the same time that have nothing to do with one another considered work? We may as well bring the dictionary into this discussion. The *verb* of work, as in, its act, is to: **be engaged in physical or mental activity in order to achieve a purpose or result, especially in one's job; do work.**

The goal is achievement. Thus, work has to consist of engagement in the single thing that will achieve the desired result. If we're spending time on things that do not bring us closer to our desired result, then we're not working, we're being busy, and this is a horrible state to exist in day after day, month after month, feeling as though we're genuinely working hard but we're **spending more time in avoidance of work than actual work.**

It's inevitable that we look at what others have accomplished with an envious tone, seeing a perceived *lack* of work on their part resulting in far greater success than we're able to achieve with perceptively *more time spent working.* We wonder why some seemingly do so little and yet win so greatly, while we do so much and yet don't win at all.

We, thus, come to the conclusion that there's no point. And in some light, it's true. There *is no point* of being busy. There's no point of working on things that don't bring us closer to our goal. **There's definitely no point of doing anything with divided attention.** But who ever really comes to this conclusion? It's more natural to look at our plight and have pity for ourselves than to realize that we're the ones who are at fault, and that we're focusing on the wrong things, on *everything* instead of a single thing.

Rarely do we feel a lack of meaning or purpose, nor do we feel envy or pity, when we're improving. We tend to feel these things when we are doing a lot but getting nowhere. It's incredibly difficult to get nowhere, to see nothing from your work, if you're disciplined. It's almost impossible. If you're not disciplined, however, it's very easy to do a lot of work, to put in a lot of effort and time, and see nothing from it.

Envy and pity, two cancerous and horrible perspectives, are the result not of a lack of effort, but a lack of focus.

It is not your state in life that you're sad about, but the lack of improvement to show for what you've done. I am, of course, excluding lazy people. These are useless humans who somehow haven't admitted to themselves that laziness has never won anyone a single thing. To be devoid of achievement, of meaning and purpose and actual results in life, however, does not mean you're lazy, it may mean you work very hard, but lack focus and discipline.

It's taken me a while to finally understand that how I was working for so long was an exercise in being busy and not on accomplishment or efficiency. I was, essentially, working hard at *avoiding* achievement.

The path to actually getting good work done, or seeing daily improvement, was a simple one filled with simple, obvious changes to my day and how I work. Now, I'm not where I want to be, not close, but that daily improvement we need to feel as though we're moving toward something is here, every day.

I removed social media apps from my phone. Instead of just sitting down to work, I planned my work day the previous evening to determine what would be the *best* use of my best hours. I set a timer when I do work to have a deadline and to make it clear that there's a period where there has to be a singular focus. I downloaded an app that blocks all programs on my computer except for the one I'm using for work.

Nothing magic, just the acceptance that I was in my own way and the adoption of things, habits, even apps that would make being busy for business' sake, not an option.

# Be Relentless

Tim Ferriss's *Tools of Titans* is a great book for its actionable wisdom and insights into elite performers. You can take a chapter or a person from that book and learn something that you can apply to your life every day for the rest of your life. You will see a new process, be it of problem solving or learning or working, that will completely change how you do things.

Casey Neistat, a film producer, filmer, and artist, was a surprise read for me. If you visit his YouTube channel, you'll see wonderful work, great videos, and a guy who appears to be living a pretty adventurous and free life.

The key is free. He doesn't *seem* like the kind of guy who has a schedule or ritual or any semblance of discipline incorporated into his life (the key word is *seem*, when you look at the volume of content and its quality that he produces, you know that discipline has to be at the core of how he lives). One video is about a commercial he was asked to film for Nike. Nike gave him a budget to shoot a short film, and instead of doing what Nike wanted he took the budget and traveled as far around the world with a buddy as he could until they ran out of money. It took 10 days. The video of their trip has—as of this day of writing— over 23 million views.

He appears to be a wanderer, a creative type who shuns discipline in lieu of the creative process—the muse that finds such artists in ways that it doesn't find the rest of us. Seeing his work one assumes he's more in touch with the mythical muse than the rest of us. What you don't see in his YouTube videos or commercials is that he wakes up at 4:30 every morning, seven days a week, and edits his vlog from the night before. You don't see the routine, the discipline, the habits he's created to force the muse to come when he damn well needs it to.

He falls asleep at his desk every night around 1:00 a.m. and then wakes up three and half hours later and begins again.

He's consistent. He's relentless. It's this consistency that enables him to do a ton of work and to create all that his imagination can conjure while living a pretty awesome life filled with variety and adventure.

Consistency *is* being relentless. It's pursuing something grand as your ideal, but understanding that daily persistence and hard work are the things that will help you chip away at that great, grand goal.

To be consistent you have to stay in your lane. You can't get caught up in the comparison game that claims too many a life, and far too many days. You can't jump from focus to focus trying to find the thing that will work without ever completing a thing. You need some semblance of monotonous, arduous, never-changing work in your day toward the same thing.

If I didn't work on this book every single day until it was finished, it would have taken a few years long to finish, and by that time, after having spent a few years *dabbling* on an idea, I would have likely stopped working on it because something else caught my eye, my attention, and my passion.

Behind great achievement is purposeful, persistent work. The great achievers planned, and executed. They determined what had to be done, and they did it every damn day without exception. There are thousands of untold and unheard-of nobodies who dabbled, who had a good work day, and patted themselves on the back with an unscheduled day off the following day.

Whatever you or I or anyone else wants, the acceptance that it comes only after time and work well done has to exist. If any part of us thinks that there's a way to *not* do the work and do it well and still get what we want, somehow without earning it, we have to kill that voice and never hear its whispers again.

# Be a Professional Learner

*The Practicing Mind* is one of the better books I've read, and I'll read it many times over. It's a book about the process of practice. In the myths section of this book, we went over the talent myth and how talent is actually the result of practice and interest. In *Bounce,* Matthew Syed talks about how purposeful practice made men appear as though they had innate abilities that the average or even good among us don't possess. In *The Talent Code,* Daniel Coyle writes about talent hotbeds. He shows us that hotbeds for a host of exceptional Brazilian soccer players, Russian female tennis prodigies, and Renaissance-era Florentine artists provided a higher quality kind of practice for people who were keenly interested in what they were doing.

Great thinkers are focused on the practice that creates the ideal, not necessarily on the ideal itself. Dreamers and wishers and envious folks love the dream, the goal, the place in the sun, but they don't like practicing. Practice, however, is discipline, especially in our age of distraction. Rather than aiming to become a professional whatever, aspire to become great at the craft.

There are things that force you to focus on the process more than others. I've taken up archery and shooting, and both require you to be in the moment. If even for a second your mind wanders, the result suffers. Focus completely on doing, however, and the end result is typically a successful one.

Free throw shooting in basketball is another example of something where a focus on the steps, on the process, generally leads to a successful result. Focus instead on the result, and you end up with a missed shot. When I'd walk up to the free throw line, I'd focus on the body movements and how I wanted my hand to finish and where the ball should be each step of the way. This helped me increase my free throw shooting percentage more than 20 percent.

Golf is another potentially frustrating activity that requires focus and can be painful if you have a wandering mind.

Good practicers are great learners, and great learners discover things that pass most of us by.

Practice requires disciplined focus that cannot include your phone or the Internet. It cannot consist of more than one thing, or more than one thought, or more than one tense.

What's meant by *tense*?

You cannot become great at practicing while thinking of the past or the future. There is only one time frame for your mind, and that's the present.

## Deep Work

Cal Newport's book *Deep Work* is a must read for anyone who wants achievement and freedom gained from living a disciplined life. Newport suggests using "time blocks," which are something I've adopted over the past year that helped me remove this facade of being busy and replaced it with intense work periods filled with improvement and accomplishment. No more intention, it's been replaced by action, largely thanks to the adoption of work or time blocks.

A time block is a period of time blocked off for a single activity. This necessitates that you establish an environment with only a single option. I, for instance, shut off my Internet when I have scheduled a writing time block.

This also necessitates that you know how long you're able to focus on one thing without distraction. Start small. Set, say, a thirty-minute block aside to focus on a single thing. Shut off your phone and Internet and anything else that may distract you, and set an alarm for the end of your thirty-minute block. You'll be astonished at what you can accomplish when your focus is singular.

You'll notice that as you practice purposeful deep work, your quality of work and your ability to focus improves. Increase the time span of each block, from thirty minutes to forty and so on. It's believed that the maximum a person can focus on a single, challenging task, is 90 minutes. Beyond that, you'll find that your attention waivers. That doesn't mean that you can't continue working on the same task, but the quality and intensity of your ability to focus will diminish. Moving on to another task following a brief, active restart can be the remedy.

Between each time block, I do something active to get the juices flowing and to get out of the mentally drained state I usually find myself in at the end of a lengthy period of focus. I also find that my early-hour work blocks are more effective and longer than my work blocks later in the day. You have to know what your magic hours are and schedule accordingly.

If the goal is to get shit done, do everything you can to get the best 'shit' done that you're able to do, ending each day having won a small battle in your overall war of achievement. Time blocks have helped me do that, and as I've mentioned, I've spent a lot of time being busy, but since adopted strategies like this I'm getting more done in less time and the stress, worry, and utter lack of pride in what I was getting done has gone away.

If you're getting real, measurable work done on tasks that are important to your overall goal, you're going to feel well, peaceful, and proud by your day's end. It's hard to feel down or even depressed when you're accomplishing things, when you're improving, when there's clarity in why you're here and what you're here to do.

Adopting Newport's *Deep Work* practice of using time blocks will help you in a few ways:

1.   You'll get more work done in less time, which should be the goal. Why spend more time doing less productive work? It makes no sense, yet that's what most of us do.

2.  You'll enjoy your life more. Getting work done makes you a happier human. When, at every day's end, you have *proof* for your being here for a good reason, you feel a deep sense of pride and accomplishment that remedies the blues often brought on by our tendency to compare our life with that of another. Furthermore, you're going to have more time to actually do the things that make you feel alive *outside of work*, and with the people you'd most like to spend time with.

3.  Lastly, you'll be better able to maintain clarity and ward off the stress that comes from worry. When you habitually focus only on a single thing, whether it's work or something else, you fully engage in that thing without engaging in the thoughts of *what else* has to get done for the day, or your life, to be successful. Thus, you're able to do more in less time, you're able to have more fun while doing it, and you're able to maintain the clarity necessary not only for achievement, but for living a good life.

Time blocks should not be confined to work. This idea of distraction-free time should infiltrate your family time, your exploration and play time, your training and lifting heavy things time. Have a block where your phone is checked, your e-mail is answered, your favorite website visited, and duplicate this block in short spurts throughout the day. Don't, though, allow tasks that represent what you want now and not what you want most creep into time blocks where your focus should be singular and directed only at tasks of importance.

# Our Dying Appreciation for Consistency:
## Why Most People Are Consistently Inconsistent

We touched on this briefly in talking about being relentless. Being consistent isn't something that most would deem 'flashy'. Consistency, to many, seems boring, it seems like it's a state that *opposed the verb of living* as they'd like to live. The truth, of course, is that consistency is necessary for any worthy achievement.

What's bizarre is that most people are consistent, they're just consistently *inconsistent*. They're consistent in that they routinely quit things before they're completed, or they continually change their focus in life and in work. They're consistent in that they consistently don't know what to start working on, or what they should give their time to, or what time they wake up and go to bed and when or if they go to the gym.

We're all being consistent. Some are consistently effective and efficient and successful. Others are consistently ineffective, inefficient, and thus, consistently unsuccessful.

It's more difficult to be consistently efficient, which is why most don't do it. It takes effort to shut that part of our brain off that doesn't want to do what needs to get done, a part of our brain that, for most of us, wins a majority of the battles. We do what we *feel* like doing rather than what we have to do if we're going to gain the life we want most.

What happens, though, when you begin to create routine and habit is that being consistently successful eventually brings you success. It also becomes a lot easier when something becomes a habit.

Peter Thiel, the billionaire investor and cofounder of PayPal, cited two people when asked who he thought of when he heard the word successful: Elon Musk and Mark Zuckerberg. More surprising than the *who* was what it is about these two men that sticks out for Thiel. They are, in his eyes, consistently relentless. They attack day after day and will likely do so until the day they die.

Being successful can't be finite. It's not something you are one day and not the next. It is who you are. To accomplish something on a grand scale, you cannot merely go through the motions or dabble. You have to *live* this stuff, this high achievement lifestyle. You have to do the right things for a long time. This consistency isn't something you're born with, it's something you can develop through planning and discipline.

When you look at high achievers, consistency is the thing that stands out as a commonality among all of them, and a lack of consistency, or a lack of doing the things that got them wealth or power or success, typically stands out as a commonality for their downfall - if it ever comes.

The goal every day is to have to crawl to bed because of the energy you've spent during the day. You've burnt your candle completely. Tomorrow, thankfully, you get a new candle.

Do not, however, seek the discipline of consistency thinking that it's something you can turn on momentarily, acquire when you want, and then turn it off. Consistency gets easier as momentum builds, and as you see the results of the momentum of work you've put forth, but momentum can be lost in a day, a week, or in minutes.

You need to, however, build the momentum in the first place. You have to practice focusing on a single task or getting up at the same time daily or planning at the end of the day. Doing it once or twice or waiting to do it when you *need* to do it, won't work.

In *Deep Work*, you read about highly productive individuals, including CEOs, authors, and innovators, who get a ton more work done than the average human but who often do so in little time. They create freedom with discipline. What they do might not consume their entire lives, but when they are doing it nothing else exists. Your work, your family, your time have to own your attention.

Earlier, you created your ideal vision for your life. You're not going to realize it if you're not relentlessly, consistently the man your ideal needs you to be. You can't do this in a half-assed manner, and why would you want to? Why in God's great name would you want to *live* in a half-assed manner? It makes no sense. You can live, giving everything you have to every day, or you can exist, wandering and wading, forever staying in life's shallow end.

What Thiel noticed in Musk and Zuckerberg is something we all have access to. It's a passion for life, for a project, for a career, for a craft, for a way of living that we have to become absorbed with if we're going to become what and who we want to become.

When you dissect the lives of some of the world's great performers, you realize that it isn't innate talent or a God-given gift that makes them great. It's a recipe consisting of one or more of the following attributes:

**They're consistently more excited about the problem they're trying to solve than anyone else.**

This has a lot to do with their vision and much to do with their worldview.

Take Theodore Roosevelt, for example. This is a man who did more work in his lifetime than many of us could do in a dozen lifetimes.

How?

It didn't have to do with any one thing that he was pursuing because he engrossed himself in many diverse areas. He was a relentless hunter who hunted big game all over the world. He was an explorer who mapped out new channels of the Amazon River after his presidency was complete, a time when most tend to rest or write, not do something so dangerous and deadly. He was a prolific writer who penned 37 books (by my count, I may be short on that). He was the President of the United States. He was a rancher. At some point in his life, he was probably something that you'd like to become.

**He was not passionate about a single thing but instead passionate about a number of things.**

He loved the strenuous life and detested being static. When he focused his attention on something, he would accomplish it without without deviation but would eventually deviate to something else and give *that* his entire attention. The constant would be his forward movement.

His tenacity had a lot to do with his idea of time and life. His view that life should be strenuous, not easy, led him to constantly be on the move or engaged in some kind of project.

What's incredible to me is the fact that he didn't *have to* extend himself like this. He was born into wealth. He could have sat back and enjoyed where he was born and who he was born to. He didn't. He burnt his candle everyday of his life, or close to it.

If we're waiting for life to happen, we're going to spend an eternity waiting and we'll never actually live our best life. Roosevelt lived because he vigorously pursued whatever piqued his interest.

This isn't easy to do, but it can be done, starting with the steps in this book. It begins with a vision for your life, followed by a daily routine and schedule, and is realized through persistence. Begin. Please don't wait any longer. Worms are getting closer to being our nightly bedmates, and yet we spend our time on things that don't align with who we want to be or the life we want to live or with what excites us.

Roosevelt was a man of incredible action, and this was nothing more than a choice on his part. He wasn't born with more energy than the rest of us. He was a sickly child who seemed destined to be confined to a life indoors in his bed. His father stepped in and changed the trajectory of young Theodore's life when he put him on a training regimen that included boxing and, long before it was popular, resistance training.

His father saw that the path to freedom from illness for his son was through pain not rest, as so many doctors had prescribed.

Pain is something the majority avoid. Yet, it's the very thing we need for improvement. We need the discomfort, the physical pain that comes from training our bodies to be stronger, to endure longer, to withstand more. We also need the pain of failure and rejection to learn and evolve.

> **To live life in safety's comfort is to guarantee**
> **that you end life in regret's embrace.**

Relentlessness is not enticed by mediocre goals. You will not relentlessly thirst for knowledge in an area that bores you. You will not rise early if your quest doesn't challenge you. You will not persist and endure inevitable trials if your goal isn't important to you.

As Theodore Roosevelt so brilliantly stated:

> *Far better it is to dare mighty things, to win glorious triumphs,*
> *even though checkered by failure, than to rank with those*
> *poor spirits who neither enjoy nor suffer much, because they*
> *live in the gray twilight that knows not victory nor defeat.*

**The best moments in life are immediately after the butterflies** that invade your stomach and make you think that maybe you shouldn't do whatever you're about to do. Those butterflies are not a deterrent, they're a compass telling you exactly what you need to do right now.

Think about it. Maybe it was when you were about to ask out your future wife for the first time, or right before your wedding or proposal. Butterflies should act like a flame at the end of a match being held at the end of a fuse that's attached to a stick of dynamite. Let the flame come in contact with the fuse. Always let that match light the damn dynamite.

I live in Calgary, Alberta, Canada. If you don't know anything about the city, it hugs the Canadian Rockies. As such, adventure lies near, very near, but you still need to get off your ass to go experience it. The beginning of the Rockies is a 40 minute drive from my house. To get deep into the mountains you're looking at 1-3 hours. My favorite fishing spot (I'm new to fly fishing and fishing in general, but I have a wonderful spot I go to weekly) is a 40 minute drive through some of the most beautiful country you'll ever see. You still have to get off your ass and drive. I don't *always* do it. But I go most times I plan on going and one of my triggers for going is if I don't feel like doing it.

I've never been on a hike and not had an awe-inspiring experience. I've never been fishing and not had the same. The activity is always worth it. The barrier is often laziness and wondering if it's *going to be worth it.*

Over the years I've learned repeatedly that if you don't feel like doing something, you should probably just do it.

The feeling of butterflies is an indicator that you must act, this feeling that whatever we might want to do, or even have to do, isn't worth doing, is a sign that it is. It doesn't matter if its chores or hunting, doing always feels better than not doing and accomplishing *anything* feels a hell of a lot better than not doing so.

**Daring and decisiveness are the qualities of winners.** Both take work, practice, and awareness. I used to see things that I did not want to do and didn't feel like doing and I wouldn't do them. I allowed my feelings dictate my actions, which is a horrible way to live. Feelings are often lies, which is frustrating because we've begun to attach so much meaning to them.

When you think about your final days - something that we should contemplate over often - these inactions that fill our lives, these moments where we decide *it's not worth getting off our ass and getting out there* become even more stupid. They're not just useless, but genuinely stupid when we realise what's done instead of the thing we'd decided to do. It's always the best choice to just *go*. Regret is worst in what's *not done* than in what *is done*.

You choose to be relentless, to act on the butterflies, to say "no" to the feelings of laziness. You do not see such action as pointless because when you get off your ass and do something there is always a benefit, there cannot *not* be a benefit, especially if there's struggle involved.

**Instant gratification isn't a thing. It's not
a focus, a desire, or an option.**

*Everything can be taken from a man but one thing: the
last of the human freedoms—to choose one's attitude in
any given set of circumstances, to choose one's own way.*

—*Viktor Frankl*

Neither the elite performers nor the producers in flow or deep work had entitlement issues. Feelings of entitlement prevent you from persisting long enough to realize your dreams and to become who you can become if you fail for long enough.

Entitlement doesn't always present itself as the screaming child who didn't get what he wanted, or the recent graduate from an elite university who has to start at the bottom of a company that they somehow think they should be running. Entitlement can set in slowly. It can be created after years of failure and a lack of achievement. Oftentimes it comes up when we've genuinely worked hard, but haven't won. We look outside of our lane to the accomplishments of others and we begin to *feel* (again, the lie of feelings comes up) as though we deserve what we have not earned.

Entitlement is delusion, and it's delusion that prevents happiness, meaning, and achievement. It's a cancerous thought process that cripples potential.

You really have to watch how you think and be truthful in where your thoughts are leading you. If, for some reason, you think you deserve more than what you have or where you are, stand guard. This is different than thinking you're *above* or better than your current situation. You likely are. Your potential means that you're *a lot better* than where you currently are and that you can do a lot more and live a much more successful life, but that's different than thinking you *deserve* more. You don't. I don't. To deserve is to earn. Wherever we are is what we've earned. If we want something better, we have to earn it, and earning happens when we do the right things for a long enough time.

Entitlement creeps into our brains when we think we deserve what we have not earned. Stand guard against such thoughts, they can potentially ruin your life.

**The cold, hard truth about accomplishment is that each of us is where we deserve to be.**

To remove any idea that you're entitled to something that you have not earned, there are a few books you should read. One of them is *Thoughts of a Philosophical Fighter Pilot*, by Jim Stockdale. It will show you that leaders and winners find things that they can control even in circumstances where control seems beyond them. Stockdale graduated from the US Naval Academy with a bachelor's of science in 1947. After more than a decade of naval training and service, he began training as a naval pilot, in 1949, ultimately serving as a test pilot until early 1957. In 1959, the navy sent him to Stanford University, where he delved into the Stoic philosophy that he credits with helping him survive seven years as a prisoner of war in Vietnam.

He then graduated from Stanford in 1962 with a master's in international relations. Preferring fighter pilot to academic, he was sent to Vietnam. On September 9, 1965, during his second deployment, he was shot down over North Vietnam and captured by the Vietcong.

The torture meted out on American POWs was notoriously brutal. The Vietcong set out to remove pride and humanity, to break men physically and, more, mentally. They sought to deprive POWs of their dignity, bribing them to betray their country and, in the process, themselves.

In his book *Good to Great*, Jim Collins writes about something coined the Stockdale Paradox, which can be defined by two statements from Stockdale:

> *I never lost faith in the end of the story, I never doubted not only that I would get out, but also that I would prevail in the end and turn the experience into the defining event of my life, which, in retrospect, I would not trade.*

It's necessary to have faith in what is not known. The paradox arises in how some people attach dates and details to the unknown, clouding it with an illogical and irrational sense of hope. The POWs that broke weren't necessarily the pessimists, who saw the horrible situation they were in, but the optimists who chose to cling to an ignorance of reality that would eventually break them. In Stockdale's words,

*They were the ones who said, "We're going to be out by Christmas." And Christmas would come, and Christmas would go. Then they'd say, "We're going to be out by Easter." And Easter would come, and Easter would go. And then Thanksgiving, and then it would be Christmas again. And they died of a broken heart.*

This destructive form of optimism is a dismissal of reality much in the same way entitlement is. In not facing where you find yourself, your reality, and in not accepting where you are as the truth, you have no foundation to build upon. You're not aware of the battle you're facing in the present, which is a dangerous line of thought to follow.

Stockdale writes in *Thoughts of a Philosophical Fighter Pilot*:

*George Bernard Shaw said that most people who fail complain that they are the victims of circumstances. Those who get on in this world, he said, are those who go out and look for the right circumstances. And if they can't find them they make their own.*

Entitlement and irresponsible optimism both ignore reality. They're the feelings and thoughts of men who want to avoid the stressful circumstances of the present and dream about a scenario that is not in their control. You can no more control the date you get out of a prison camp than you can control the date your business succeeds. Yet, there were men in Vietnamese prison camps who dealt with their reality and even found meaning in their suffering, who found lessons in their unjust, painful, and horrific situation. These were ordinary men like you and I who showed an extraordinary ability to create their ideal through persistence in facing and not avoiding truth and reality.

**Man's greatest accomplishments have come
as the result of extreme pressure.**

To avoid that pressure, to feel as though you're entitled to peace, prosperity, and opulence when that's not your reality, is to deny yourself of one of life's greatest opportunities and lessons. In his book, Stockdale talks about the biblical story of Job, which gives a good understanding of the world.

Job was once a prosperous man, happy and successful but struck by terrible misfortune. He loses sons and daughters and servants and all of his worldly possessions. He's infected by disease. He ends up sitting naked on an ash heap scraping his flesh with potsherds, asking, "Why me, O Lord?" He believes that the Almighty has allowed or even caused such calamities to befall him. He's a good man. What has happened to him makes no sense, bears no justice.

God doesn't answer as Job anticipates. He does not acknowledge Job's virtue or agree that the situation is unfair. He instead points to the awesome dimensions of the universe and asks Job if he could do anything like that. Could he create the heavens and the seas? Where was Job when God created heaven and earth?

Job doesn't answer. He bows his head and puts his hand over his mouth in the silence of faith, of endurance.

The lesson that Stockdale takes from Job is simply that *"life is not fair. There is no moral economy or balance in the nature of things such that virtue is rewarded and vice punished. The good man hangs on and hangs in there."*

Do not diminish the power of perseverance under pressure. Do not rob yourself of such a virtue. Socrates said that **"Courage is endurance of the soul."** To think you deserve more than what you have now, to feel as though you're entitled to more praise and worthy of more money and prestige is to ignore the necessary battle you face. You must endure the test, the pressure, like a man to gain from it the vital lessons of courage and grit and toughness that only it can provide.

Stockdale was intent on gaining something from his years of imprisonment. The sheer, brutal pressure of torture provided him with clarity, toughness, and wisdom that few have.

The same can be said for Viktor Frankl, the author of one of my favorite books, *Man's Search for Meaning*. He created his views of the human process, his form of psychiatry called logotherapy, within a Second World War Nazi Concentration Camp. Much like Stockdale, he saw that some found meaning in their suffering; that others wished they were elsewhere, and it killed them; and that a few maintained whatever ounce of control they could to choose their attitude toward the horror around them.

I write this to help with an understanding that the world is far from fair, that we may find ourselves in horrific and completely unfair circumstances, but that we must accept them as our reality. We must accept what is but also understand what we can control. To feel entitled robs you of the ability to accept what is, and it thrusts you into an envious mood, a cynical look at the world and at who wins and who loses. Entitlement is weak, it's evil, it will make you quit.

You cannot compare your path with someone else's. You cannot compare what you have with what someone else has. We live in an age where comparison is rampant. It can hit us when we step outside and see the new truck our neighbor has bought that we so enviously want. We're also faced with opportunity to compare our lives with the lives of others every time we turn on our phone, our TV, our computer, or our tablet.

Today it can seem difficult to avoid the desire to compare who we are against who others are, what we have with what others have. It isn't.

1. Don't ignore what you have, what's good in your life. At every day's end or beginning, write down three things

that you're grateful for that have happened within the last twenty-four hours. It's an exercise that will change how you look at your life. It's also easy to be blind to what we have, especially in comparison to what we had.

An easy example is the journals I keep. I keep them so I can, far too infrequently, review them. I've kept every journal I've ever had. I've lost a few, but most are somewhere on my bookshelf in my office. A couple years ago I hit a bit of a rough spot in my business. Everything seemed to be flat. There was no growth, no grand ideas, things felt stale.

For some, unplanned reason, I opened up an old journal, one I had written in my very early twenties where I mapped out what I wanted to accomplish and where I wanted to be. In short, I was, essentially, there. I had a new house that I bought before my 30th birthday (one specific goal I had), my business was doing well over six figures, and I even had 'my dream dog', a dogo argentino named Teddy. I had travelled to Italy, Argentina, and South Africa, which were all on my list.

Had I not opened that specific page in my journal I would feel as though I had done nothing over the past 5 years.

Feelings are rarely honest and true. Sometimes, of course, they are, and we should follow them, but the feeling of not doing something because you don't feel like it is rarely what's best and what's good for your life. The feeling as though you've done nothing, that you have nothing, that you lack potential, is particularly evil because it robs you of the good and contaminates it with the bad.

2. Don't spend time on social media. Simple. It's not healthy to look at the life someone else is living. You'll inevitably compare yourself with them, think that you're just as talented and worthy as they are, and then feel depressed by what you have and feel as though you're entitled to more when you're not. You may *think* you're being motivated by the yachts and mansions, the ranches, the accomplishment of another, but somewhere in your mind and soul you'll *wish*, and wishing kills happiness and the potential for fulfillment.

What's even worse than wishing is the feeling that, by watching the lives of others, you somehow deserve what they have and have earned.

## It's the Pursuit That Provides

Life isn't a mountain, or at least you shouldn't expect it to be a mountain.

The fable of Sisyphus is applicable here. Sisyphus was the incredibly cunning founder and king of Corinth. His greatest triumph came at the end of his life when Hades, god of the underworld, came to claim him for his kingdom of the dead. Hades brought along a pair of handcuffs. Sisyphus was able to convince Hades to demonstrate the use of said handcuffs on himself. And so, the god of the underworld was kept in a locked closet at Sisyphus's house for many days, which put the chain of being out of whack, preventing anyone from dying.

Finally, Hades was released, and Sisyphus was ordered to report to the underworld for his eternal assignment. Sisyphus was again able to avoid death by tricking Persephone, the queen of the dead, after which he again lived on for some time.

Eventually, his cunning ended and he was hauled down to

Hades, where he was condemned to an eternity of pointless labor. He was to roll a great boulder to the top of a hill, only to have to repeat the process ceaselessly because the boulder rolled back down each time.

Self-improvement is essentially pushing a boulder up a mountainside that never ends. It's those who can love the pain, the struggle in the moment and avoid looking at the hopelessness of the future or even of their surroundings, that will take something from the pain. Those who don't or won't, will learn nothing, gain nothing, and remain as nothing.

It's therefore the process, the daily discipline and focus that you should love and not the place you want to get to so you can feel good about yourself and post nice pictures of what you've earned. Admittedly, it's a difficult state to get to, though it's not complicated in the slightest. In fact, being in this state removes the choice that is stress from your life (the bad kind not the good kind, the kind that is improvement). This state removes envy and worry from your life.

Elite performers are who they are every day. They don't stop. They're relentless, not just in doing things but in figuring out what single thing deserves most of their time or their best hours to yield the biggest result.

That's the simplicity of it. You do not have to rise to the occasion in a single moment, to do something grand or great, you simply have to be as good as you can be everyday. The trick is to point yourself in the correct direction - whichever direction you damn-well want - and then live every day as if it's a life of its own. Be good. Do good. Don't lose concentration. Don't be lazy. Work hard. Work hard on a single thing at a time nad complete it.

History is filled with men who've worked incredibly hard for long periods of time and didn't achieve what they wanted. Keep in mind that the work is often the reward and that the reward you are aiming for may be a finality that doesn't deliver the meaning and enjoyment that you'd hoped for. So often our quest brings us the most joy and meaning; don't discount it.

Sure, you have to work on the right things. Success is never guaranteed, but self-improvement is. The only thing you can guarantee is failure by not adhering to the above principles. Many give up because they see the futility in the work. They see the pain in the present as the barrier, the thing they do not want, ignorant to the far greater pain of failure, debt, and utter regret in their future that they guarantee by being lazy.

I hope that last paragraph hits home. Writing it, did. Not that they're great words or original ideas, but in that moment of decision, where you're deciding whether to work or relax, to plan or to go with the flow, to get in the truck and go for a hike or remain sedentary, remember that effort in the present isn't for the present, it's for the removal of future despair and for the acquisition of future pride, happiness, and freedom.

*If you want to be free tomorrow, work your ass off today.*

## CHAPTER 6
# How to Be Successful

## Pain vs Pleasure

*Adversity doth best induce virtue...*
*while luxury doth best induce vice.*

—*Sir Francis Bacon*

Most people live off their earnings. By month's end, they're at zero. No matter how much they earn, a little or a lot, most Westerners live this way.

John D. Rockefeller, the first oil tycoon and once the wealthiest man on earth, did not live like this. He was born poor, and while his old man was swindling people all over the eastern United States, eventually shacking up with a second family, John D. had to take care of his mother and seven siblings.

He was also very religious, which both hurt and helped his desire to acquire wealth, depending on how you look at it. It helped in that he saw gaudy living as sinful. He saw opulence as waste. Even when he had earned millions, he acquired fewer possessions than his counterparts. He didn't dress like a millionaire. This distaste for excess helped him keep more of his money than others and use it to earn even more money, avoiding the pitfalls of success that test a man just as ruthlessly as failure.

It could be argued that his religion hurt his accumulation of wealth in that from day one Rockefeller tithed. He didn't start tithing when he was rich. He tithed even when he had little to give. He gave 10 percent of his gross earnings to churches, even to help smuggle escaped slaves from the south before, during, and after the American Civil War.

There are many keys to Rockefeller's ascendancy as the world's wealthiest man. He was smart, he forged sound partnerships, and he pinched pennies. Throughout his life he kept meticulous personal and business ledgers of income and expenses. He found ways to cut costs in his life and in business that helped his bosses earn more, then his partners, and ultimately his shareholders. Early on, he found that by bringing all business services—plumbing, barreling, and so forth—in-house he could save money, which allowed him to buy more and gained him more credit from creditors, who knew he'd pay them back.

**It wasn't the birth lottery that led Rockefeller to become wealthy. It was discipline.**

Rockefeller turned his back on the things that other wealthy persons aspired to and built an empire over time. Most millionaires earn and preserve their millions in very much the same fashion. They acquire wealth through astute business dealings and by budgeting, investing, saving, and avoiding frivolous purchases. In so doing, they gain freedom from financial stress.

Some people, however, strive for wealth solely to own nice things and end up broke. A few among the wealthy seek wealth simply for the freedom it grants them from financial worries and from the social trappings that keep people in a perpetual state of victimhood.

You have to be truthful about your desire to acquire wealth and power. Does it stem from a deeper desire to own more than your neighbor, to prove others wrong, to one-up your peers? Or do you want wealth because it gives you the freedom to help, to live, and to avoid the pain of debt?

Once you earn more than enough to pay the bills and feed your family, the process for accumulating wealth is there for you. You can't, however, benefit from the principle of compounding if you relish buying things over the freedom of wealth.

It's a choice, stuff or freedom. This choice will shape your life.

The crippling financial stress that hangs over people often isn't due to earning too little but in spending too much. When it does stem from earning too little, the path to earning more—as you'll see—is rooted not in innate talent or the birth lottery but in discipline, in drive, in being relentless. You cannot earn more acting like those who earn little. You have to change who you are, how you think, and the way you make decisions if you're going to rise to a new standard of living.

For people crippled by debt but earning more than enough to cover monthly costs, the financial stress is similarly self-imposed. It's fuelled by a desire to fit in, to feel value in the present from a purchase whose charm quickly fades and is replaced by need of yet another ostentatious purchase.

Most of us have enough to live well and are often seduced into thinking that buying more will make us feel better. It doesn't work like that.

Discipline will help you earn more and keep more.

# Keep Your Goals to Yourself

## A Powerful, Unconventional Habit

Hidden in the recesses of my wallet is a torn, discolored old check for 100 million dollars. The check is written and signed by me to me. The writing is clear and purposeful. You can tell I had every intention of cashing it before it expired. I wrote the check to myself at the advice of some self-help book I was reading in my early twenties. It's dated for this year.

I have nowhere near 100 million dollars and only six months to cash the check. Crap.

To be honest, I loved the exercise. It made me feel like I'd accomplished something great before I'd actually accomplished anything.

Think about that.

We're told to shout our dreams from the rooftops, that by saying something it makes it more likely to be accomplished. The truth appears to oppose this often-held view of self-help books and motivational speeches. We are not meant to proclaim what we have not yet done. It gives us a feeling of reward that we have not yet earned.

I was introduced to this idea when I stumbled upon a TED Talk by Derek Sivers, a serial entrepreneur and the owner of one of the most insightful blogs online, sivers.org. Sivers' TED Talk, *Keep Your Goals to Yourself,* lays out the premise that goals should not be announced before they're achieved and that there's research dating back to the 1920s to prove the value in this.

Peter Gollwitzer, a psychology professor at NYU, has been studying this phenomenon since his 1982 book *Symbolic Self-Competition.* More recently, he's published test results in his research article, *When Intentions Go Public: Does Social Reality Widen the Intention-Behavior Gap?* His findings shatter the advice of almost every self-help book you've laid your eyes on.

Four different tests of sixty-three people found that those who kept their intentions private were more likely to achieve them than those who made them public. Those who conveyed their goals to friends and family gained only the psychological reward of proclaiming a goal or a dream before it's achieved.

Siver's talk, Gollwitzer's findings, and a wonderful article on sivers.org called "zip it," speak of the identity symbols we have in our brain that are triggered by actions and words. These identity symbols make up our image of ourselves, and since actions and thoughts create symbols in the brain, talking about our goals and dreams causes us, as it says in "zip it," to "neglect the pursuit of further symbols." In other words, talking about dreams tricks our brains into thinking we've done the actions that our dreams require.

I've never shown the check in my wallet to anyone. Yet, by writing it and carrying it around I have to admit I felt like it was achieved. I've found this with other goals as well. Saying them feels like accomplishing them. It puts me in the mind frame that they're already completed. But the truth about goals of any importance or value is that they're difficult to achieve and most often are achieved only by the man who persists, not the man with the head start in life.

Self-help books are heavy on this idea that we should talk about what we want to achieve. But that's too easy, too simplistic. It may feel rewarding to talk about what you want to do but haven't yet done, but I'm asking you to have the discipline to bite your tongue, to be the one guy at the party who doesn't blurt out his sales forecast for the next quarter or what he thinks he can earn with the launch of a new product or what he's saving up to buy or the book he's intent on writing.

Simply put, shut up. I'm saying this to myself as well as to you. Work in silence. Work hard. Let the achievement be its own proclamation.

# You Are Who You Are Trying To Become

*For success, like happiness, cannot be pursued; it must ensue, and it only does so as the unintended side-effect of one's personal dedication to a cause greater than oneself or as the by-product of one's surrender to a person other than oneself. Happiness must happen, and the same holds for success: you have to let it happen by not caring about it.*

—*Viktor Frankl*

Excellence is a habit. To be who you want to be, you have to set the rules that define the man you aim to become. That is how you progress. You become who you are. It's as simple as a decision made and as clear-cut and final as a direction chosen. You do not continue as you were, with your bad habits, lazy behavior, and weak and limited mindset and outlook about what's possible in life. You become the man you aim to be by following the rules he would need to follow.

We think that this self has to exist at the end of something or as the result of something that we currently do not have. I'm the same, I've always thought that *one day* I'll become the man I know I can become when I finally reach the level of success I've always wanted to reach. It's such a stupid way to think of it, to be brutally honest with myself. To *push* the man that success depends on to a time when the success is won, is idiot. *Of course* you have to become the guy that is worthy of the achievement before you achieve. To do otherwise is like trying to build a house without a first floor.

We think that when we get what we're after we'll change. The truth is that change can occur in a moment, with a decision, a plan, and a course of action. We need to evolve, to become who we *can* become, now, because *then* doesn't happen without that evolution today, right here and right now.

Benjamin Franklin understood that the wealth he wanted was dependent on who he was, the way he lived his life every day. And so he set himself rules, or virtues, based on what he wanted to accomplish and who he wanted to be.

The line of thinking, and it proved to be a correct train of thought, was so simple and effective, yet rare. He defined virtues and rules that, if followed, would help him become the man worthy of what he wanted to achieve. Rather than focusing on 'a break' or a helping hand, he instead decided to define who a successful man was rather than what he has, and then live as that man.

Defining your own rules for life allows you to become successful even before you've achieved success. It makes your daily decisions in the battle of what you want now versus what you want most, black-and-white and crystal clear.

Too often it's a lack of clarity on what decision to make that derails us. By having rules for your life and virtues that guide your decision-making, this clarity barrier is removed. You can then act as the man who will acquire the wealth, the skill, the life you dream about living in the present and no longer have to wait to become him.

The virtues that Benjamin Franklin established for himself kept keep him on the best-possible path to his goal. They prevented him from deviating from that path. As you read Franklin's virtues below, have your ideal you in mind. Which of his virtues can you adopt, and which of your own would you rather implement? Make your own list, asking always, what virtues bring me closer to my goal and what virtues do not?

If you do not have guiding virtues, you do not have principles that show you how to live. You then are open to influence. There are too many bloody influences in our society today that pull you away from who you want to be and who you want to live as. Why would you leave who you are and the man you live as to chance when it's something that should be completely under your control and defined by you and you alone?

## Benjamin Franklin's 13 Virtues

1. **Temperance.** Eat not to dullness; drink not to elevation.

2. **Silence.** Speak not but what may benefit others or yourself; avoid trifling conversation.

3. **Order.** Let all your things have their places; let each part of your business have its time.

4. **Resolution.** Resolve to perform what you ought; perform without fail what you resolve.

5. **Frugality.** Make no expense but to do good to others or yourself; i.e., waste nothing.

6. **Industry.** Lose no time; be always employed [H76] in something useful; cut off all unnecessary actions.

7. **Sincerity.** Use no hurtful deceit; think innocently and justly, and, if you speak, speak accordingly.

8. **Justice.** Wrong none by doing injuries, or omitting the benefits that are your duty.

9. **Moderation.** Avoid extremes; forbear resenting injuries so much as you think they deserve.

10. **Cleanliness.** Tolerate no uncleanliness in body, clothes, or habitation.

11. **Tranquility.** Be not disturbed at trifles, or at accidents common or unavoidable.

12. **Chastity.** Rarely use venery but for health or offspring,

never to dullness, weakness, or the injury of your own or another's peace or reputation.

13. **Humility.** Imitate Jesus and Socrates.

## Accountability

Discipline without evidence is useless. That is, you have to see how you're doing, demonstrate your progress. You cannot just think that you're disciplined, especially when it comes to something as abstract as virtues.

You can think you're improving, but without principles to live by and a process by which you measure them, evidence of your improvement will take too long to show itself, which can lead to discouragement and a destructive lack of consistency.

In my fitness business, I see this far too often. Guys don't track their results, they get bored, they see a shiny new object (another program), buy it, start it, then hop to another one a month later. Their goal, the muscle they want to build or strength they want to develop, takes a couple years to achieve. My shorter programs sell more, but my longer programs that last a couple years and are billed monthly (forcing guys to act on what's laid out for them or risk wasting $50 a month) yield better results.

Persistent consistency is a necessity for any goal, and quite often we can achieve it by avoiding every new tactic or hack that comes our way. We can also track how we're doing to see the fruits of the process instead of waiting for a vague feeling of accomplishment amid our changing standards.

We have to track both the process and the result. That is, if we define our virtues we have to hold ourselves accountable, along with tracking our performance in our work or business or any other area of life we want to improve in.

Our faith must lie with our principles, our rules, our virtues.

We have to understand that adhering to them means that we're becoming the man our ideal needs us to become, that it will only be a matter of time until we are that man, and that the goal that was once a pipe dream is our reality. Thus, they have to be *good*. We can't just write down whatever the hell we *think* we need in the moment. They have to be true to who we are and who we want to become.

Some want to become tougher, stronger, and more powerful, in which case check out *the Barbarian Virtues* (www.thebarbarian-virtues.com). Others want to become kinder, more caring, and so forth. Really dial in and think about *who* your ideal is. Don't think about who you've been *told you are*, but who you admire in the present and in history and what characteristics and virtues would help you rise to that caliber of human.

If you want to achieve anything without getting derailed by problems or catastrophe's as most people do, you will need to develop toughness and grit. If you want to acquire wealth you'll need to both study and adopt a frugal lifestyle. If adventure is a necessary aspect of your idea of a life well lived, then you'll have to become courageous.

Understand the truth about what you want, make sure it's grand, and dig deep into the man - who he is - that can and will achieve it. Define his virtues and attributes and live them religiously. And keep track of how *well* you're living them. Track not only the result, but the process that will get you the result.

Without principles and a system to track them, evidence of success often only comes in the form of your final victory. That can take a lifetime to realize and may come in a form different from what you envisioned. And so, you need to track your progress and your end result.

Progress is measured in the daily process of your work. Improvements lead to the result. If you're not sure you're improving with your process—and the proof may not always show itself as more money earned or more eyes on your website—you might be inclined to too often switch focus, alter your routine, and adjust what you're working on.

**By measuring yourself not by an income goal or the growth of a business goal, which can take weeks, months, years, and decades to attain, but by who you are every day, you ensure your personal growth, which is what your overall goal and mission is dependent on.**

The life you want to create for yourself and your family isn't dependent on anything but you. If you improve, the likelihood of having your desired life improves.

Franklin understood this, and he created a framework to grow with.

Just as we need a program to build a better body, we also need a program to become better men and to live better lives. This is why having virtues to live by is so incredibly important. **They tell you who to be.**

As a guy, you may not be fond of being told who to be. But you are constantly being told who to be regardless of whether you decide on the virtues that make up this archetype or someone else does.

Every day, you read billboards, articles, books, and ads and watch shows that tell you who you should aspire to become. More often than not, these sources are telling you to be someone that makes them money; namely, a consumer.

It is vital that you take control of this narrative and lay the framework for who you want to be in the present to become who wish to become and to create the life you want to lead. Otherwise, you join everyone around you in following every whim and desire that enters your consciousness.

In financial terms, you will gain a better grasp on your spending because what you buy must align with your virtues. You don't simply buy what others lay out for you. You don't purchase things you desire in the moment. People without virtues find that the battle of whether to buy or not becomes a battle between their emotional self and their logical self, and the logical self rarely wins. In terms of work, you'll pursue projects that fit with your virtues, with who you are and how you act. You'll focus on the things that push your business forward not on momentary desires that have no place in your calendar. Your work thus becomes more efficient, not because you're smarter, but simply because you have principles that guide your actions rather than desires that pull your attention and focus.

Your relationships also benefit from your having principles, rules, or virtues that guide your daily actions. You will become the man that your lady deserves—if she's the right lady—and desires on a primal and emotional level. Women want security. As a man who knows who he is and where he's headed, you'll give her both the financial and the physical security she needs to live her life to the fullest, which will, in turn, allow you to do the same.

Following is an example of how Benjamin Franklin laid out his virtues weekly and of how he tracked his adherence to them daily. This chart is easy to generate. I've also supplied some templates in the tools section you'll find on the website thelostartof-discipline.com/resources.

## Benjamin Franklin's Chart of 13 Virtues

| VIRTUE | S | M | T | W | Th | F | S |
|---|---|---|---|---|---|---|---|
| **Temperance**. Eat not to dulliness. Drink not to elevation. | | | | | | | |
| **Silence**. Speak not but what may benefit others or your self. Avoiding trifling conversation. | | | | | | | |
| **Order**. Let all your things have their places. Let each part of your business have its time. | | | | | | | |
| **Resolution**. Resolve to perform what you ought. Perform without fail what you resolve. | | | | | | | |
| **Frugality**. Make no expense but to do good to others or your self. Waste nothing. | | | | | | | |
| **Industry**. Lose no time. Be always employ'd in something useful. Cut off all unnecessary actions. | | | | | | | |
| **Sincerity**. Use no hurtful deceit. Think innocently and justly. Speak accordingly. | | | | | | | |
| **Justice**. Wrong none by doing injuries, or omitting the benefits that are your duty. | | | | | | | |
| **Moderation**. Avoid extremes. Forbear resenting injuries so much as you think they deserve. | | | | | | | |
| **Cleanliness**. Tolerate no uncleanliness in body, clothes, or habitation. | | | | | | | |
| **Tranquility**. Be not disturbed at trifles, or at accidents common or unavoidable. | | | | | | | |
| **Chastity**. Rarely use venery but for health or offspring; never to dulliness, weakness, or the injury of your own or another's peace or reputation. | | | | | | | |
| **Humility**. Imitate Jesus and Socrates. | | | | | | | |

For a great Benjamin Franklin Journal check out
artofmanliness.com

*Image taken from 13virtues.com*

Virtues cannot remain in 'thought land', they have to be brought into reality, boiled down, defined, and transcribed. We *think* we know what we stand for, but unless we define it and find a way to measure our adherence to it, to them, we go back to living as we were, which is typically *not* in line with how we *want to be living*. There's the standard that is who we have to become to create the life we want to create, to accomplish what we want to accomplish, and there's who we're living as now. **We cannot go on living as anything *but* the man we need to be to get what we want to get.**

Franklin defined the virtues that his ideal self would need to live by, the virtues, that if lived by would get him what he wanted to get, and then measured his adherence to each of them. That structure he put in place is powerful, it acts as an accountability system that's unrivalled. It forces you to be truthful about who you are and how you're acting, and it measures your progress not in comparison to someone else's journey or plight - which is always a dangerous, destructive way to go about improvement - and instead to your own ideal and idea of who you ought to be.

A chart like Franklin's to show us that we're improving and adhering to them makes these virtues more than just ideas. They become actionable things whose doing or not doing gives us either positive or negative feedback.

We need feedback. Motivational and inspirational quotes make us feel good in the moment, but they will not result in achievement and continual success. Persistent excellence, will, and we can ensure that we're acting out persistent excellence by grading our behavior in relation to a predefined ideal.

Thus, rather than waking up and 'doing our best' with no real definition of what our 'best' is, we can wake up and know very clearly what a success Chad or Bill or Bob or Hank acts like, thinks like, and lives like, and then do our best to act accordingly.

Here's a groundbreaking idea: **you are not perfect the way you are.**

To think you're perfect is to believe that you do not need to improve. That's true arrogance. I can't call a man who talks a big game but then works his ass off, arrogant, because his words are backed up by the understanding that no, he is not perfect just the way he is and he has to work hard to achieve what he wants to achieve.

**I would argue that you are put on this Earth to improve.** You were not put here to remain as you are, to be static. *To live* is a verb that requires you move toward an ideal. So choose a direction that's worthy of the gift that is life and head toward it every damn day of your existence.

You can go through your life ignoring that fact. On the other hand, you purchased this book because you agree that you can be better and you're begging for a way to get there.

Hold yourself to a higher standard. Give yourself feedback. Lay out the principles or virtues that will guide how you make decisions and how you behave, and you will create the process by which your most audacious goals will become your reality.

**Your choice in life is simple: you're either disciplined or you're unsuccessful.**

Discipline works. It's the leveler of playing fields. An abundance of it can make a poor man rich and a lack of it can make a rich man poor. That's what's so wonderful about discipline; every one of us can develop and possess it. It's an attribute of strength and control. When your peers are slaves to their desires, you're in control of your fate.

# CHAPTER 7
# The Society of Slaves

*Advertising has us chasing cars and clothes, working jobs we hate so we can buy shit we don't need. We're the middle children of history. No purpose or place. We have no Great War, No Great Depression. Our great war is a spiritual war. Our great depression is our lives. We've all been raised on television to believe that one day we'd all be millionaires and movie gods and rock stars, but we won't.*

*—Chuck Palahniuk, Fight Club*

Most people enact little control over what desires they pursue or ignore or suppress. Most don't even know that the majority of these daily desires should or even can be ignored. They see fulfilling these desires as an expression of who they are and therefore good and right.

From a young age, we're told that that we're special. The reality is that every one of us needs a lot of work, to become better fathers, husbands, brothers, and men and members of society in general, let alone to move closer to what and who we are aspiring to become.

The problem is that desires have become something society views as good. Freedom has come to mean giving into desires and not controlling thoughts, ideas, and emotions.

**It begs the question, how can someone be free if they're a slave to their desires?**

They can't be. It's silly and ignorant to think so. If you see your desires as the source of freedom, ask yourself if you can truly say "no" for the greater good, for the thing you want most over the thing you want now?

If you can't, you've accepted that you're powerless and that no matter how destructive the desire, you can do nothing to free yourself from its grasp.

Yet, we're told to chase our desires in the moment regardless of whether they fit into the overall desire we have for how we want to live our lives and who we want to live our lives as.

**To be considered good, a desire has
to improve you or your life.**

Eating chocolate whenever you want to isn't *good* because it leaves you fat and unhealthy and likely with rotten teeth. Watching porn whenever you want to isn't good because it leaves you impotent, distorts your view of women and of sex, and can ruin a relationship. Smoking isn't good because it kills you. Buying whatever you want isn't good because it leaves you broke.

Both porn and purchasing are similar. They give you a brief dopamine rush that provides momentary pleasure. But that takes away from the success you want in your life. Giving into either of these desires simply because they'll make you feel good for a moment is shortsighted. It's also handing your happiness over to an act and a thing that you can, essentially, replicate on cue. Your life, then, becomes more about pleasure than meaning or purpose or accomplishment, all the things necessary to live a flourishing life and to feel as though you've lived for some good reason other than just breathing.

A society where we consume for the sake of consuming or to feel better about ourselves is a slave society. You are a slave if you depend on some external thing to feel better, especially when they're things that take away from your meaning, purpose, self-worth, value, and ability to maximize your efficiency. The desire becomes your master.

A man cannot be led by desires and lead. He cannot be a victim to distraction and win.

## Happiness Cannot Be Your Pursuit

You're pursuing something, a goal, wealth, success, whatever. The pursuit has to be some kind of achievement, something to hold your head high about. The pursuit cannot be happiness. Happiness is an emotion, and one that's been put on far too great a pedestal in modern culture.

Happiness has rarely been the pursuit in successful societies. Improvement through effort, persistence, and hard work, has. When pleasure and mere happiness become the focus, civilizations like Rome, fall. What brings success will bring happiness, but what brings happiness won't necessarily bring success. Thus, the focus must be success. Happiness can be the result of the achievement, but if it's the only and primary focus, you're putting all of your ambition and energy and effort on something that's fleeting, that's subjective, that isn't real or tangible or necessarily earned.

What you pursue has to come as the result of effort and persistence, it has to be warranted, earned, not given. Even if you win the lottery, you still need something to chase, some ideal you aim to hunt down, a goal that scares you because of the scope of what you're going to have to do to achieve it.

Those who pursue happiness will one day wake up and feel a deep void, something missing from their lives, a real reason to wake up, something that demands effort. We need achievement like we need air. Happiness is nice, but it's rarely dependable.

## Urgency

American entrepreneur, venture capitalist, and author Peter Thiel, who founded Paypal, has an outlook on goals and their time frame that helped him accomplish incredible things in a short span. He reviewed his most ambitious, long-term goals and realized that he didn't have to wait. No one has to.

In fact, by pushing your goals into the far-off future you're also delaying the actions that must be taken to achieve those goals. And that may well result in your failure to achieve anything.

Goals demand action, and action requires a deadline and the urgency that comes with a deadline. It's the urgency of studying for exams the night before rather than months before that *forces* intense focus. When you bring your greatest goals into an immediate time frame, you're forced to take the goal seriously, to live to a standard that will help you get what you want.

Want to quit your job and start a business? Set a plan that you'll start working on now, today, and that will culminate at the six-month mark.

Want to travel the world but can't quite do it yet? Book a trip for six months from now and then hustle to make it happen (I've done this, I booked a 3-month trip to Italy, and when I booked it two months before the plane left, I couldn't afford going but worked to make it happen, what a wonderful fire lit under me arse).

Want to move your family to a different country, buy a house, write a book, build an online empire? Six months!

For most of my life, I've followed the goal-setting practices that most of us are taught. We set long-term goals, then shorter-term goals, and finally some immediate-term yearly and quarterly goals.

Fuck. That.

By the conventional method, the massive goals I want to accomplish, including this book, were set so far in the future that they didn't seem real. They were dreams, and I liked dreaming about them, which is a horrible thing because it makes you feel like you're doing the thing but you're not taking it them seriously enough to accomplish them. A ten-year goal does not force you to reassess how you spend your time, what your habits are, and what actions you're taking every single day, neither do five-year or one-year goals.

Six months, on the other hand, is scary. It puts real urgency into what you want to accomplish and, more importantly, it makes you hyper-focused on the daily details, the immediate disciplines that you have to develop to create what you're aiming to create.

Scary is good. Ten years is not. If I look back at goals I set ten years ago, or even five years ago, the tracks I was to follow have been long deviated from, even forgotten. I'm on a much different path than I was back then, which is why the vision that you create should be brought to a more immediate time frame. I don't even set annual goals any longer. I'm done with them. They permit us to relax. We do not need any more permission to put off who we need to become to create what we want to create. Set your ideal, then figure out what you can do right now to get closer to that ideal.

Six months is eminently doable, provided you use your time well. Just think about what you want to create, not the reward from that creation. That reward—money or acclaim or whatever—cannot be realized without doing the required work and may be out of your control. The project is something you can control and complete within six months.

Six months is real. It's close. You can tangibly imagine it and the fear-induced discipline you're going to have to develop to meet this deadline.

If all you have is a dollar amount that you want to make, it's a wish. To make things real, ask what task, what project you have to complete and complete well to make that dollar amount or how much you have to put away every week to invest to create the wealth you want to create.

Focus on the process, the project. This is under your control. The reward is nothing without it. You cannot achieve a single thing if you create nothing.

### It's Never Been Easier to Be Successful, Just Look at the Competition

It's important to understand the masses. They're not go-getters. They're not hustlers or workers. They watch entire seasons of TV shows in a single sitting and call into work for a sick day because they see it as a right.

The competition for success, for happiness, for greatness, and for accomplishment has never been weaker. It's like running a marathon against obese people who think being obese is who they are and thus something they should be proud of, not something they should fix. It's who they are and who they are is an accomplishment in and of itself, without need of improvement.

You, conversely, seek improvement. You read. You work. You rise early and hustle. You train to be great at life, and like never before your training will yield results in a capitalistic society that still thrives off of competition, no matter the contrary thinking of the masses. So although working for work's sake without much thought about what you're working for isn't great, it's still a lot better than what most people are doing.

You have an insanely unique opportunity in today's society. There are more ways to succeed, more avenues to get you what you want than ever. There are also many more potential customers, and they love to buy things.

Your competition is the 99 percent, which displays small to mediocre thinking and miniscule action and effort. You're not competing with the 1 percent, the winners; they're doing things that the 99 percent can't comprehend because the 99 percent don't believe success is theirs to have.

You do. You see that discipline is the path to whatever you want from life. You see that correct action always eventually brings results. All around you, meanwhile, you have to admit that people are increasingly entitled. They view people who work and win with envy and hate and not, as you do, as inspirational.

**It's never been easier to win. If you take your ego out of it, understand the myriad of paths to victory, avoid living someone else's dream, and apply discipline, there's very little competition that can derail you.**

Your competition is yourself. You cannot hold yourself to the standard of the masses, that's downright depressing. Hold yourself to a higher standard, the standard of who you are trying to be, and you can't but win if you persist.

To be sure, there seems no end to the number of people after the same thing you're after. But they're not disciplined. They don't act like winners. They're TV watchers and gossipers, whiners and spenders, enviers and wishers. They aren't actually your competition. The only person you have to be better than is who you were yesterday. That's it. You know that person intimately. You know where you have to improve and that you have the power to improve every single day in your areas of weakness.

Forget about everyone else. Understand yourself. Know how

you can improve and improve. Know your weaknesses and fix them. Know the lies that are fruitless desires and rid yourself of them. Stay in your lane. Beat who you were yesterday.

**It's a great time to be alive, and an even better time to be ambitious.**

# CHAPTER 8
# What Do You Need to Be Disciplined About?

*There is no easy way from the earth to the stars.*

—*Seneca*

When I took a leap in my early twenties or so and walked into a boxing gym, I got my first experience in a sport that to that point I'd only enjoyed from afar, as a spectator. I loved boxing even before I stepped into the ring and got punched in the face.

One of the first things I remember my old man giving me was a *Sports Illustrated* VHS videotape about the life of Muhammad Ali. My mom told me stories about Rocky Marciano. I read books about James Braddock well before *Cinderella Man* opened in theaters. Unfortunately, I ended up at the wrong gym initially. The fella there knew a lot about boxing but wasn't licensed and couldn't get me a fight. He taught me a lot, but he kept my progress slow. We moved from punch to punch in snail-like fashion, not because he wanted to teach me the perfect punch but because he figured the slow pace would delay my desire for a fight.

I got wise to him and jumped to another, very different gym. I'd never sparred at the previous gym; jabs or crosses only, no full on sparring. My first day at the new gym, the trainer threw me in the ring to spar.

I got my ass kicked.

The only punch I was really comfortable throwing was a jab, which was fine for keeping the other fella off but not for doing damage or providing him with the myriad of angles needed to defeat a good fighter. I walked out of the ring with two black eyes and a busted nose and a more profound love and respect for the sport of boxing and the struggle it involved.

Back to discipline...

The purpose of this book is to solve the root of your problems. Your desire to lose weight, for example, isn't a matter of genetics or the right workout but of discipline, with diet and training. Your desire to get rich and possibly marry an absolute knockout isn't dependent on chance, on an idea, or on luck but on your ability to discipline yourself to be smart and effective and to get a lot more done than your competition.

Everything we want in life is won through discipline, no getting around it. A lack of discipline denies you the opportunity for happiness, meaning, purpose, pride, self-worth, and accomplishment.

You feel better about yourself when you're disciplined. You're able to accomplish more, earn more, save more when you walk your own path.

Discipline is the solution on many levels. It's more than avoiding the wrong things. It's choosing the right things, where the right things are the things you really want, not the things that society tells you to want or that your desires beg you to chase in the moment. Discipline brings clarity and the ability to create the object of said clarity.

When I began boxing, I knew I'd have to be more disciplined.

I thought that discipline would be tangible, literal, and mainly physical. I'd have to get up early to run. I'd have to eat the right foods, especially when I was cutting weight. I'd have to get in better shape, work harder, avoid booze and partying, and study fighters from the past.

I did all of those things with relative ease.

I love to train. I love to fight. I love the feeling of eating healthy foods, the energy they bring, the results they give. That's easy stuff. You may struggle with this kind of thing, but changing that is easy and simple, as we'll discuss in the next chapter.

What I didn't realize was the importance to boxing of a level of disciplined decision-making that many of us aren't even conscious of. I'm much more aware of it now after my exploration of Stoic philosophers and philosophy, other philosophies, the Good Book, and so forth. I'm especially cognizant of how significant this level of decision-making is to every aspect of our lives.

Within our daily lives there are thousands of decisions that shape our day and how we look at life. We can quite literally choose who we are by making disciplined decisions that are guided by our vision of who we want to become.

This is a deeper aspect of discipline. It's a mindfulness with a purpose on an unconscious level that can change your life and who you become.

I played two primary sports growing up, hockey and basketball. Both meant a lot to me. So much so that I never played as well as I could have because of the pressure I placed on myself. Ambition and imagination had a crippling effect on my performance.

Age, too, played a part. I was too immature to see outside myself, to detach and realize the scope of what I was involved in. I was playing a kids' game. That reality never sunk in. These games were the focuses of my life. Everything I wanted centered on them. I took that weight into each game, and although I'd play well I didn't play on par with the skills I'd developed through the hours of diligent practice I'd put in. I killed it in practice, but not in games, not consistently.

I loved boxing to the degree I loved hockey and basketball. The difference was, I was old enough to put its importance into perspective. I was more aware of my line of thinking, so I was able to focus on the moment, not on whatever dreams I had in the sport while I was fighting. Boxing forces you to do that though.

During basketball games, my mind wandered. I'd think about the future and what could happen if I played great, and my play suffered. In boxing, it's pretty hard to think about anything but the fella in front of you trying to knock your block off. But still, it took discipline, particularly amid fatigue and pain, to keep my mind in the moment and, above all, to enjoy the moment.

The last fight I had was against a fella from the States. Everything went wrong. He showed up overweight. He was just a bigger guy than they told us he was. But lying is common in boxing; anything to get an edge. He was also a southpaw, another convenient oversight on their part, and I hadn't trained with any southpaws. This is a big thing because facing a southpaw calls for a different fight strategy and completely changes your strategy if you didn't know your guy was a lefty and you haven't faced a lefty before.

We found all of this out minutes before the fight, when we saw him warming up. I was in good but not terrific shape myself. What stood me in good stead against this fella was that I walked into the ring with a mental discipline that helped me focus on the right things and have fun. I fought a great fight, winning each round, dropping the guy once, and coming away with a decision.

## The Discipline No One Talks About

Discipline and clarity go hand in hand. To be disciplined about the right things you need to be clear on where the line needs to be drawn. But drawing your line in the sand isn't always an obvious task.

## *A Disciplined Mind*

Our thoughts dictate everything we do and how we see the world. We can think positive thoughts, winning thoughts, losing thoughts, lazy thoughts. Most people think of themselves as victims in some way, likely not intentionally. This passes control of their lives to some bad entity they feel is responsible for their lack of success or happiness: parents, government, birthplace, teachers, whatever. Someone or something to blame allows them to avoid accepting responsibility for every single facet of their lives.

The potential to adopt this negative thought process occurs in seemingly insignificant decisions we all make daily. We encounter countless forks in the road where we can take the path of control or the path of the victim. Whichever path we take shapes our worldview and either feeds or crushes our ambition, our ability to focus.

On a micro level, for instance, the decision to check your Facebook page during a scheduled time block versus focusing on the work you're supposed to be doing is a massive decision with far-reaching implications. **The more you move from work to distraction, the more you reward yourself with a nonwork stimulus.** You get a weird sense of joy seeing what others are doing on Facebook or Instagram. This trains you, however, to become a distracted human and deprives you of your ability to produce high-quality work.

A much better decision would be to train yourself to avoid checking your email and social media accounts and focus on the task at hand. Regardless of which you choose, you're training yourself to be efficient or to be inefficient. Think about achievement and high-achievers. Their success essentially boils down to efficiency. Most people I know have good ideas. Only a few people I know are good at focusing and carrying out those ideas and not getting distracted while they do it. These are the successful ones.

The more efficient you can be in your life, the more successful you will be. And your capacity for efficiency is unknown, it hasn't even really been tested or pushed. I know mine hasn't. If we could, for example, wake-up at 5am every morning, and work perfectly efficiently without any ounce of deviance or distraction until noon, we would be a decade ahead of where we currently are. When you look into the research about the time people actually spend productively working, you find a sea of survey-focused data that probably can't be completely relied upon, but the narrative is consistent in that it appears that people spend 3-hours or less every day productively working. If you can work efficiently - and you can - for 7 hours, something that everyone *can do*, *has the time to do*, and *ought to do*, you're immediately more than doubling what you can accomplish versus what everyone else can accomplish.

Remove external comparison and focus on yourself. Try this:

Keep a time journal of every minute you spend working versus non-working for the entire work week (if you work 7 days a week, track all 7, if you work 5 track all 5 and so on). See how much time you *genuinely* spend working efficiently. Checking articles, facebook, emails, instagram, watching TV, reading so that you're not working, don't count. Work on a project is all that qualifies as work.

Let's say you're already better than most people and you *work* for 5 hours in a day. If you can double that output and work from 5am to 4pm with an hour break, you're cutting the time you achieve what you want to achieve in HALF.

That is, you're a capable human. You have potential. Success is merely something in the future that is not yet yours, or not yet yours to the degree that you want it to be. At the pace you're going you'll get what you want in, say, 20 years, but if you double your output you'll get it in 10.

Elon Musk has an opinion on this: "Put in 100 hour weeks every week. If others are putting in 40 hours and you're putting in 100, even if you're doing the same thing, you will achieve in 4 months what it takes them a year."

Let's say you *don't* want to work 100 hour weeks, which makes complete sense. That doesn't mean that success has to elude you. It just means that you have to be more disciplined than everyone else. It means that efficiency becomes even more important because you don't want to sacrifice success, but you do want to spend time with your family or in the mountains or on the land you bought with the money you've earned, you get the point.

Just because you don't want to put in the hours, doesn't mean that you don't have to put in the work. In fact, efficiency is vital as the time you *do* put into has to be effective.

Efficiency is everything.

It's all that matters.

It *is* discipline enacted.

If, in this information age of ours, this time of distracted, you can be efficient, you open doors for yourself that are not shown to everyone else, that never appear to them. Being efficient means using your time correctly, and it's completely a choice and a muscle that you can develop.

You work. You set a timer and work while that timer is running. You do not do things that are not supposed to be done. It's such a simple concept, but if you live your life in this manner, you will not recognize the man you become. You will be shocked by what you earn. The meaning and power and sense of pride and joy in how you've lived your life will be unexplainable to the man who isn't efficient.

What you think you want now will pale in comparison to what you eventually have if you simply live efficiently.

If all you do is do what you set out to do and don't get distracted by other things, you will live a truly powerful, wonderful, accomplished and worthy life.

Call it efficiency or call it the flow state or deep work, not only is it the only way to work but it's the only way to live. The stronger your work-related focus becomes, the easier it becomes to focus and to work deeply. The more you exist only in the present, even outside of work, the less stress you have, the more you live, the more you experience what you're intended to experience rather than living in the avoidance that is being distracted, focusing on things that should not be the focus, like social media or TV or even talking about others.

The necessity for efficiency is why time blocks are powerful. Set yourself up with a challenging but realistic time. If you find focusing for thirty minutes difficult, set that as your initial goal and work up to it. When thirty minutes is easy, bump up to forty-five and so on.

## Focus!

Train yourself to focus on a single thing for an extended period of time and you're going to learn more, create more, earn more, and live better.

Leave everyone else to be plagued by distractions while you build the discipline that immediately gives you a leg up on your competition. Let everyone else in society jump from career to career in an effort to find themselves or what they like. Maintain discipline and resist the desire for constant change in preference of establishing the life and career you want.

In her book, *Grit: The Power of Passion and Perseverance*, Angela Duckworth proves the benefit of persistence. **The career doesn't matter. Meaning can be created in any occupation if**

**you decide to become the best at what you do and look for ways to improve at *what you do*.**

This push to 'follow your passion' is nonsense, because passion is often fickle. Our ideas about what we like, change.

Find something, anything. Try and get really good at it, and the passion will present itself. Don't seek passion because it's an unpredictable barometer.

Challenge yourself, push through the discomfort or distaste for an unsatisfactory job, and think bigger. Learn from it what you can. Forget sexier professions. They're often whimsical and leave people worse off than people who stick with it, persisting in a career and coming out on top.

Don't think that because there are options they need to be taken. Stay the course and take from it everything you can until something bigger and better presents itself. That said, most of the wildly successful entrepreneurs I know discovered ways to improve what they did, started their own companies, and made a lot of money.

They focused on what they did, even though they were working for someone else, and then finally broke off when they saw the need to give the world and their customers a better service than their boss could give.

## Too Busy to Be Successful

*Beware the barrenness of a busy life.*

—*Socrates*

Busyness opposes productivity, and productivity is all that matters. No one cares about the hours you put in. I've learned this time and time again. I've worked tirelessly on products, programs, and new ventures, that yielded nothing.

The market doesn't care, customers don't care, potential customers don't care. Yet many of us ambitious folks put being busy atop our list of priorities, whether we're aware of it or not.

Results are what matters. If you're busy on the wrong things, you're moving yourself away from the results you need, not closer to them.

So the decision is over being productive or being busy. We're trained, of course, to see being busy as admirable. This undermining view needs to be replaced with the discipline to see productivity as the laudable choice.

This past Christmas season, I walked around with butterflies and a weight on my chest. There were so many things to do, but I got little done each day. I was not prioritizing, something I'm ordinarily good at. I was as useless as an ashtray on a motorcycle. I worked *hard*, but I failed to properly identify where my effort should be directed. I was focusing on low-priority things and so busy being busy that I canceled plans with my sweetheart; worked late almost every day, including Christmas Day; and was overly stressed after a week of working so damn hard on essentially nothing. I was trying to do everything instead of tackling a single important task at a time, which is never a fruitful course of action.

It took a few days to realize what was going on. I stepped back and, from a detached perspective, defined my critical tasks, pushed the noncritical to later, and went to work in a more purposeful and focused manner.

In one day, I edited the book, filmed three videos for the YouTube channel, and managed to reduce my e-mail inbox to zero. I also took my lovely lady out for dinner, enjoyed a walk with the pup, and worked out.

There's a time and place for everything. You just need to figure out the place and time for your tasks before you even think about working on them. And you cannot give time to more than a single thing, it's a useless act that bears no fruit.

Being productive requires planning. Being busy requires intentionless movement. Time taken to plan, to identify right tasks from wrong tasks, to give a single task the correct amount of attention, is *never* time wasted. Time spent doing work for work's sake without thought about whether or not it's the right work *does* often result in time waste, or at least time not spent as best it could be spent. By focusing on one thing at a time, you'll accomplish this. By practicing slower movement, you'll accomplish this. By removing the option for distraction, you'll get done what must be done and avoid doing what doesn't.

This desire to be busy can be difficult to break. But it must be broken.

We have it so ingrained into our psyche that we equate success with commotion, but motion for motion's sake does nothing but move you in the opposing direction of achievement.

At every day's end you should feel as though you won. Do you?

Over the period I mentioned above, I didn't. I wasn't at peace at the end of the day. I wasn't proud of what I did. I was stressed about what I *didn't* get done. It's a crushing feeling. **I worked hard but I didn't feel the pride that should come from work well done because it wasn't work done *well*, it was merely effort devoid of result.**

Maybe you've felt the same.

You've given a lot of effort to the day, but you didn't look back at the end of the day with pride and happiness and satisfaction. Somehow, with all of the effort you gave to the day, you feel *worse*, more stressed, consumed by more worry than you did when you started.

That's not how it *should go.*

That's not how it *used to go.*

When humans were farmers and hunters and little else, what we had to do during the day was typically singular, it was routine. We had to harvest or milk the cattle or butcher the animal or feed the animals. We had to fix the fence or find food for our family. We had only a few things to do and doing them was often a matter of survival.

Today we have a lot that we can do, and whether we do one thing or another, by day's end our survival isn't usually in question. That doesn't, however, mean that by doing anything or everything that we're doing the right thing. The goal of the day is no longer about survival, but about accomplishment, meaning, purpose, and pride.

We need to do the work that gives us such feelings. Our lives are no longer on the line in the immediate, but the more we do the right work in singular fashion, the better our lives will be over time. Being that the negative effects of doing the wrong things aren't so immediate as they once were - when the man who didn't bring home dinner for his family over a long enough period put both his and his family's lives in danger - the importance of what we do isn't as drastic. Simply *doing*, working, giving effort becomes the goal. "If I work hard enough I'll be rewarded." We all *know* that's not true, and yet we don't spend enough time deciding what work must get done.

This is important.

Being busy does not make you more happy, it doesn't make you feel like you're accomplishing more, it doesn't make you feel more pride in who you are. It merely adds stress because no matter how much effort you give, you don't seem to improve.

The solution to feeling stressed, even down, at the end of a work day is threefold:

1. You have to define what you want most in life. Then you have to determine what you have to accomplish to get it.

2. You have to spend time the day before determining what task is most important, and which can be done later, and

then you have to **give them order**. That is, do one, and *then* do the next. Do not aim to do them all at once.

3. You have to do whatever you need to do to ensure that you tackle one thing at a time, completely without distraction and without your attention being divided in any way.

**Discipline is the permission to do important instead of unimportant work.**

You have to give yourself that permission. You have to allow yourself to break out of the powerful pull of society's advocacy of busyness.

Just as the carpenter ant has his singular job and does not aim to be something he is not, define who you are and what you are - audaciously so, of course - and be it alone, nothing else. A comedian's quest is funny. An author writes books. A father protects, provides, and presides (thank Ryan Michler for that one). A pilot flies. An entrepreneur creates. An adventurer ceaselessly seeks the unmundane. Define what and who you are are be that thing in a singular fashion.

**Stay in your lane.**

We can get a glimpse into what others are doing today without knowing anything of the backstory. We just see what they want us to see. We can visibly look at what hundreds of people want us to see in the run of a day. We can exist outside of our own lives and partially in someone else's.

We can. But we shouldn't.

Man, this is a struggle. There's so much opportunity to compare who we are to who someone else is, or where they are in life to where we are, or what they've done with their lives to what we've done. It's *so* easy. It's at our fingertips daily. But we cannot do this. We cannot spend a second in comparison mode. We cannot *think* about looking at what others are doing or where they are or what they've done. We have to stay in our lane not only so we can do what we're here to do, but so we can appreciate where we are, love who we love, and focus on *our* purpose.

If we spend time outside of our lane we rob ourselves of the good in life. We instead alter our perspective to be one that's inevitably envious or jealous or resentful or entitled or, and this may be worst of all, a perspective that has pity on where we are and why we're here.

Do the work you need to do. Take care of the people you need to take care of. Be the best you can be. Don't spend any time outside of your lane.

CHAPTER 9
# The Power of Habit

*The first and best victory is to conquer self.*

—*Plato*

Most of us want to be disciplined so as to avoid or to do something. Either way, we want discipline so that we can have freedom.

We all have something that we don't completely control. It may run our lives, edging into addiction, or it may just stand in the way of who we might be without its weight dragging us down.

Getting rid of this crutch or roadblock is necessary. No matter how small or insignificant, removing something that holds us back has to happen, the sooner the better.

The important thing to remember when identifying something you want to rid yourself of or develop is that it's just a habit, and habits can be formed or replaced at will. You're not doing anything epic here. You're simply replacing a bad habit with a good one. You're showing awareness of a decision that sent you down the wrong path and putting in its place something new and good that puts you on the right track.

Most bad habits are readily changed. Some, such as laziness or envy, may take more work and different approaches. But these are all just bad habits that need to be replaced with good habits.

And you have to keep in mind that this is all on you. You developed the habit. Only you can reverse it. No one can change a habit for you. You have the ability to change any of your habits, if you want. Within you there is enough strength to do this.

Only when you start thinking that you don't have this strength or start behaving like a victim who thinks he isn't in control does the habit own you and do you lose. When you feel sorry for yourself, your ability to change is lost.

## Draw a Line in the Sand

Draw a line in the sand that delineates in stark contrast between what you're doing and what you want to do, between a bad and destructive habit and the good and productive habit that you want to replace it with. That way, if you go down a wrong path you'll know so quickly and be better able to stop yourself. Without clarity deciphering good behavior from bad behavior becomes an impossibility.

Here are three things to know to become a man of disciplined habits:

1.  There is no tomorrow.

    Don't look at your life or goal in their entirety. Be process oriented and concern yourself with developing the habits you want, today, right now.

    People often lose sight of the arduous battle involved in curbing a longtime habit. It's preferable to focus on the present for overall happiness and because it allows you to care only about making one correct decision instead of looking at possibly thousands or millions of correct decisions.

This is something we have to constantly be aware of. No matter where you are, if you're ambitious, you're likely far from where you want to ideally be. Focusing on where you want to be, however, can cloud the importance of what must be done now, today, in the present. And these present tasks don't always seem grand enough or worthy enough of your ambitions. I get it. I've been there and I frequently go back to that mindset, that there's *something else* that should be done or that needs to be done other than the path I've set out for myself.

This line of thinking makes it tough to stay the course and to remain focused. Part of it's good in that we should always be aware and open of and to new opportunities. That said, I need to write this book. I've committed to it. By jumping to another project before this one is complete I'm robbing myself of the eyes that wouldn't otherwise know about any of my books or products or programs or courses because this entry point into my world wasn't given to them.

Too much time spent thinking about the massive mountain in front of oneself can be discouraging, leading to inaction rather than the action that must take place. All that exists right now are the tasks that need to be done today, the plan that was set at the beginning of the quarter, the week, and at the end of yesterday's work day.

2. It gets easier.

You form habits intentionally or unintentionally over the span of your life. In other words, you're either in control of forming them or not. It's preferable to be in control of forming your habits, but either way it takes from 60 to 100 days for a habit to form.

That's it, just a maximum of 100 days for something to become habitual. This is important to note. If you're in control and have consciously chosen to form a habit, each day within the habit-forming span of 60 to 100 days makes your choice easier to become the right choice. Just get over the initial hurdle. That's all you have to do. From there, it gets easier.

Developing the habit of waking early is a clear-cut example. I wanted to get more work done and at a higher quality. I realized that mornings are best for writing, which is a massive part of my day, so I decided to wake up earlier than my usual nearly 6:00 a.m. I sought an added hour and a half of distraction-free time, when no one would be calling or texting or expecting a return e-mail. My goal was to wake up at 4:30 each morning.

When something is habitual, a trigger, such as an alarm, is not needed. But forming habit calls for triggers. Every five days, I reset my alarm fifteen minutes earlier than the previous five-day period. I could have made this change every day or two, but five days allowed me to acclimate to and even make the new wake-up time my norm before experiencing another fifteen-minute reduction.

I had to go to bed at the same time every night or risk not having a good sleep (a sleep schedule was the only thing that alleviated my protracted insomnia). Within weeks, I was waking up at 5:15 a.m. After a month, I was up at 5:00 a.m. and rising before my alarm by the end of that five-day stretch of 5:00 a.m. wake-ups.

Finally, I achieved my 4:30 a.m. goal and after a couple weeks was by habit waking at that time. My body was accustomed to waking at 4:30 a.m. and didn't need an alarm to trigger it, which remains the case to this day.

The more you do something, the easier it gets and the less you'll crave the alternative habit you've replaced, such as sleeping in, eating junk food, or spending money on useless stuff. Focus on incremental improvement, and you'll change how you 'naturally' think and behave.

The other side of this coin is acting on the new habit. You may think it's 'tough' to get up earlier, but it isn't. The reality is, you just do it. Your choice is to either do it or to not do it. Simple enough. That starkness gives ownership over the decision to do or not to do to you, and no one else. If you don't *really* want to wake up earlier and you've set that as your goal, but you actually like sleeping in, accomplishing little, being angry that you didn't win the day by day's end, you're going to sleep in. So think about who you want to be, the life you want to live, and understand that being lazy can lead you to have a horrible existence, one devoid of power and freedom, meaning and purpose, happiness and adventure.

Don't hit the snooze button.

3.  It's on you, and that's good.

    Responsibility is a great thing because rather than your success being dependent on luck or some outside force, it depends on you. Your success rests solely on your shoulders. The decision in the moment to choose the wrong path or the right path is yours alone.

    Make the right decision.

Know the difference between what you want now and what you want most.

All you have to do is *make this decision correctly*, don't worry or even *think* about the next one. Forget about tomorrow. Forget about the macro and focus only on the micro, and make the correct decision. If you slip up - and there's no reason to think that you will, you don't have to, it's not 'human' to slip up, it's a choice - forget about it. It's done. Move on and make the correct decision the next time.

## How to Erase a Bad Habit

The simplest, most-effective thing you can do to rid yourself of a bad habit is to replace it with a better one.

You have to be self-aware, cognizant of your bad habit and when it arises. If you're unaware, you can't start any action to eliminate it. Your awareness of the nature of a bad habit and of the moment a bad habit, such as a destructive desire, pops into your head is necessary for your success in removing it.

Keep in mind, too, that this is just a desire, a bad habit. It doesn't control you and can't force you to do anything. It is something that you have control over, and you wield that control simply and quickly, by asking a question and then performing an action. And the question is

**What do you want more, a current desire or
the life you envision eventually living?**

That's the only question you need to ask. The choice is dependence, failure, and being less than you can be or choosing a higher standard, choosing victory.

The action, of course, depends on the habit you want to break and who you are. The simplest action I use to break a bad habit when it arises is push-ups. I need to do something active when I sense that habit, something that gets my mind on muscle and off the habit I want to break.

Again, though, it depends on what you're trying to curb.

When I let my email list know that I was working on a project to help guys become more disciplined, I got a ton of feedback, including specific habits many of you are trying to break and replace with something beneficial. We'll go through the most common of them here.

## Sleeping in

Most of us want to get up earlier but struggle with doing so. The solution is to simply make a choice to get up as early as you want for as many days in the week as you want and to follow that choice with the action of rising out of bed the instant your alarm rings.

That's what you can do and ideally will do but what few will do.

So start with a time you know you can wake up at. Wake at that time seven days in the week ahead. The next week, drop that time by fifteen minutes, followed by another fifteen minutes the week after that. Continue doing this until you're awake at the time you're aiming for.

This is the long approach. What you'll find is that by the time you reach your desired wake-up time you won't need an alarm. You'll often wake earlier. Keep in mind two things:

1.  It's on you to get up. When that alarm rings, stand up. Do push-ups, anything to get your blood going, including splashing cold water on your face.

2. Use three alarms, not phones, alarms, each placed a distance away from your bed such that you must get out of bed to shut them off. And don't you dare miss a day of employing them; don't let there be any chance of you sleeping in. Also try keeping your phone away from you, in another room, on mute, so you don't have the desire to pick it up during the night and look at the sleep-killing blue light that emanates from its screen.

## Not focusing

An inability to focus is similar to strengthening a muscle. You've trained yourself to not focus by chasing every distraction that comes to mind, by feeding every desire that enters your brain. Focusing involves (a) removing distractions and (b) strengthening your focus muscle.

a. Use headphones to shut out the world, shut off your internet, and so on to remove distractions from your work space.

b. Set a timer for any time you want to give yourself a determined block of work time. It could be fifteen minutes or thirty minutes. I advise the lesser amount of time and building from it. Spend each day of a week focusing on a single task for that time, then, when it becomes almost easy to do, add ten minutes.

The longest you can focus completely and without break is supposedly ninety minutes. That's your goal. If you can focus deeply for that period, you're going to be far ahead of your competition, and it will be only a matter of time until you earn what you've set out to earn and likely a lot more than you could imagine.

Keep in mind that breaking focus in any way shape or form

is a break in focus and a destruction of that 90-minute goal. That is, a glance at a site, checking your email, looking at the time on your phone and so on. All of these things count. True focus is truly singular. Be rigid in how you define focus. Don't be weak or accommodating with yourself.

## Snacking on junk foods

This is a habit you must replace. The method to do so is the same as that for how to stop watching porn (which was also a very common habit that men wanted to break). Find a habit you can do immediately when the desire to snack on junk arises. It doesn't have to have anything to do with food. You can do push-ups, go for a walk, pick up a book, or, yes, replace the snack with something healthier.

You also must remove all unhealthy foods from your house. If you want to stop snacking on unhealthy foods that make you fat or impotent or weak, don't buy them! Who cares if others in your house want them? This is a habit you have to break, for their sake too, and their cravings shouldn't change that.

## Watching porn

We essentially covered it above. First, head to yourbrainonporn. com to understand why you need to get off it and how to do so, but moving away from the desire in the moment is powerful. Find something that you can do right when that desire comes about - including real sex with your lady. As an aside, porn degrades your desire for real sex, and real sex with your lady is a glorious thing that no man should temper or quell.

Watching porn releases similar endorphins that are released

during sex, but the hormonal benefits aren't nearly as beneficial as sex with your lady, nor is it good for your personal development.

Of course the watching of porn has dramatically risen with our entitled society, where we want without earning. As I mentioned, watching porn gives you the same endorphins release or 'rewards' as does sex. And you don't have to do the work of finding a lady or getting your lady in the mood that you have to do with real sex. It's easy, porn, that is. It's weak. It's not the way of the man it's the way of the weakling. By watching it you're training yourself to take the easy path, but not the right path.

Use whatever website blocking tools you need to use to make sure you *can't* act on the desire, but also get something better in the way of that desire, an action that removes you from its grasp.

## Not sleeping well

I've had insomnia for a lot of my life, so sleeping well was long a struggle. What's changed that is a sleep schedule. I get great sleeps now.

Go to bed and wake up at the same time every single day. If you are out late with your pals one night or your lady, which is fine, you have to at least get up at your regular time. This is on you, you can do it. It's not a difficult choice once that alarm rings. The benefits in energy, high testosterone levels, and a litany of other things that result from a good sleep and regular sleep hours can't be undervalued.

A firm, set-in-stone sleep schedule is the only thing that's going to make a massive difference in the quality of your sleep. You'll also want to avoid:

1. Blue-light screens of any kind within two hours before bedtime. Your eyes need to be prepped for sleep, and screen light prevents that.

2. Booze after 5 p.m. Yup, this one sucks, but alcohol is proven to degrade sleep quality. You may feel sleepy after a glass of wine or scotch, but the depth of your sleep will be affected. What do you want more, booze or sleep? You decide (sometimes you want the booze, in which case, you still have to get up at the same time the following morning, like I did this morning after drinking a couple glasses of scotch with a cigar last night).

Do these things for a month, and you'll see a massive change. Fail to do either one of these things, and you fail. It's not genetic, it's not the world's fault for setting society up so that it messes with your ability to sleep. It's your fault, just like it was my fault. I lacked discipline in my sleep schedule and routines before bed, and when I created that discipline, the insomnia was solved. It's almost magical (wink).

## Being lazy

Effort is entirely under your control. There is no enemy in this habit except you. Lethargy shouldn't be on anyone's list, yet it's among the most common e-mail requests I get: How do I stop being so lazy?

Just stop! If you've read this far, you have all of the tools you need to do so. But the truth is, you just stop. You wake up earlier. You work harder. You set bigger goals. You stop complaining, and you stop taking the easy path.

If you've read any self-help book - even the good ones - self-talk is given heavy importance, and I *do* think it's important, but not always. Sometimes, actually oftentimes, we don't need self-talk as it gets in the way of action. If we have something planned, we should not think about doing it, we should not think about whether or not we *want to* or *feel like* doing it. Those thoughts should not enter our minds, yet they almost always do.

**If we have something planned, be it a task, a chore, whatever, we have to do it.**

Don't let your brain get in the way of your life.

Don't let how you feel in the moment deter you from the tasks you've laid out for yourself.

This sounds incredibly simple, and that's the point.

On his podcast, *The Jocko Podcast*, with guest, Jody Mitic, a fellow Canadian, but a military hero whose book you should read, Jocko is asked by Jody whether or not he uses self-talk. His answer was, surprisingly (surprising because I've never hear anyone admit this before), "no". This was a revelation to me. For my entire life I've been struggling with self-talk. I've been working at improving it, making it more positive, using it to propel my life and my mind forward.

But why?

Self-talk has its place when we're deciding what to do and which action to point our lives. We talk to ourselves in thought form to make decisions about what actions we should take.

**The key is that self-talk has its time and place.**

It should be confined to the time where you *set* your goals for the week, month, quarter, day, or year, but once the actions and tasks and goals are defined, ACT!

Shut off the self-talk and act, do, accomplish.

You have to understand that our self-talk is influenced by our emotions, which are often lies disguised as feelings, or by our upbringing and the limiting beliefs we've developed. We set our goals with daring and audacity and then the small, weak-thinking aspect of our being dissuades us from acting on them when the time comes. So, don't let it. Don't let the years of being told that you're less, or the mediocrity you've become to see as normal, get in the way of what you've set out to do.

Act.

Set your life in a direction and head in that direction.

Stop preventing yourself from living the life you've laid out for yourself as the ideal.

You are not a lazy person, you're *acting* lazy, and it's your own thoughts that are making the lazy choices. Stop listening to them. Stop giving them breath and life.

Act. Move forward.

When you have set out to do something, when you have a day planned, stick to that plan. Don't think. Do. You've already thought, that's where the plan came from. You no longer need to think. You need to do. Now, go.

## Persistence

We have too many options. We also feel as though we're entitled to the things we want in life because we've spent much of our lives hearing how important and special we are. We are the center of the universe. But, really, all too rarely do we view our lives from afar.

Imagine viewing yourself right now from high overhead. Around you can see other people working at their jobs, dealing with problems, taking care of their families. You'd see that whatever you're dealing with right now is one of many issues in your neighborhood. The higher your perspective, the more people you'll see juggling an ever-greater number of problems of increasing complexity.

When you see yourself as one of seven billion people on the planet, you are forced to acknowledge that you're not special, that you have a lot of competition, and that whatever you want in life you're going to have to earn it.

When we view ourselves as special and entitled, grit is unknown to us. If we don't get what we want when we want it, we jump ship and start a new path.

That's not how life works. Choose a path, stick to it. Find the meaning in that path. Find the good, the beauty, the opportunity. Within any career there's a need for innovation. Keep your mind open to the innovations within your job. And have a hobby that occupies your hours when you're not working.

I've been doing what I'm doing now for eight years. Before this, I was the poster boy for a lack of persistence. I loved hockey, but quit when I found basketball. I loved basketball, but quit when I found boxing. I started in corporate sales for a cell phone company, but quit within nine months. I launched a training business, but quit it. Sure, each of these things was a part of my path, but I lacked consistency and persistence in the details. What I didn't lack was persistence in the pursuit of improvement. And I think that's important.

Persistence can take many shapes and forms. You may hop from career to career for a bit, maybe from passion to passion (Google 'Mike Rowe Don't Follow Your Passion', it's perfect). Be careful, though, too much change isn't always a good thing. Sometimes, you need to stick it out and see where the path leads. And you should never cease improving. Always get up early, read, work out, and learn. Persistence in self-improvement should be lifelong.

Persistence is not a habit that occurs magically. It's on you. But here's a couple of things that will help:

1.  Forget about your peers, stay in your lane.

    Don't work to show off your accomplishments to others. Don't care what others think about you or what you're doing. Image is nothing. Some of the greatest success stories have come in people's latter years, after decades of toiling in mediocrity and learning, growing, and working. Forget about what others are doing, and do your thing. Stay in your lane. Don't change lanes and chase someone else's dream because they're doing well. Persist.

2. Remember your goals.

Read your goals daily and update them every six months. Keep them fresh in mind and ambitious enough to keep you excited about what you're doing.

Have your direction in life and focus daily on the process to stay true to that direction.

## CHAPTER 10
# The Power of Routine

*Success isn't always about greatness. It's about consistency. Consistent hard work leads to success. Greatness will come.*

—*Dwayne Johnson*

This morning, I woke up at 5:00 a.m. I did 100 push-ups, then went downstairs, filled a big glass with water, made an espresso, and sat down to write.

This is when the battle began. For the next twelve hours, I fought the urge to check websites and social media accounts and text messages on my phone. It was as if every force in existence was trying to pull me away from what needed to be done. Immediate desires for pleasure and avoidance seem far stronger than our desire to be successful, happy, purposeful, and accomplished. Our desire to avoid work and to check emails and text messages in the moment is stronger than our desire to win in life.

At noon, against every natural desire in my body, I went to the gym for an hour to lift weights and hit the bag. Howard Cosell once said, "Sports is human life in microcosm". So is a workout. Within the 30-60 minutes of training are moments where we want to take it easy, even quit. No one else will know if we take a shortcut, skip a set, even skip an entire exercise, but we'll know. Not doing what we set out to do, going easy on ourselves, kills our soul, our resolve. It diminishes who we are, our reliability, our manhood. It seems so insignificant, but the man that takes a shortcut in the gym will take a shortcut in the mountains or at work or in his marriage.

These things seem unrelated but I beg to differ. If you've ever met a man who is simply excellent, he is so in both the minutiae and the monumental. We've already covered it but it begs another mention; we are not going to rise to the moment, we are only going to fall back on our training. When we're in the gym we're literally training to become tougher, more resilient. Some miss this lesson and spend their workouts gazing at their biceps in the mirror. Others, the Jocko's, the Ali's, the Tim Kennedy's, the GSP's of the world, they take lessons from training that most gloss over. It isn't merely about building a stronger, healthier body, it's a matter of mental toughness that will help you in every other facet of life. The act of doing something that you may not feel like doing, that's painful, makes you a better man.

A workout will pit two voices against one another in your head. One wants ease and comfort, and the other—your true voice—wants pain and discomfort, those things necessary for improvement. Discomfort is necessary for growth, something that's especially blatant in the gym. When the voices start pitching their cases is when you do as Jocko does and shut them both out. **Thoughts that follow feelings can kill dreams. So don't allow them air.**

Back home after the workout, my weaker voice began to make some noise. I wanted to relax and turn on the TV, but that wasn't a part of my schedule. And I set my schedule when I was thinking clearly, the evening before, so rather than listening to this weakness reason, I shut it out and followed the plan. Today I won. I've lost so many bloody days that it's ridiculous. It's when I think, reason, and listen to what I *feel like doing* rather than doing what I plan that I get in trouble. It's a lesson that I continually have to learn which is why I want to hammer it home - you do not have to learn this lesson more than once. Don't let your feelings shape your thoughts and don't let those thoughts shape your day. Let your schedule define what you get done today, then do it. Without my schedule, I'd be lost, pulled and pushed by every desire, none of which is in line with the life I want to lead.

I don't think this battle ever ends, either. While I've only relatively recently begun to win it with some semblance of consistency, I can see that it will always exist. I'll always struggle to focus. I'll struggle with thoughts that I *deserve* what I have not yet earned. That's life. It's a battle. Accepting that it's a battle is a necessity. Ignoring that it's a battle and instead thinking that it should be easy and fruitful without too much effort is a cancerous line of thought.

**Winning these battles isn't a matter of willpower but of planning and commitment. Don't pit desires in the moment against what you've set out to accomplish. Give yourself only one option.**

Going through every day having to choose between comfort and rest and work and pain, we're likely to choose the easy path more often than the difficult one. It's our nature to choose ease.

All over the world, and especially in the West, people are choosing to follow their immediate desires at the expense of what they think they want for their lives. We do this daily. We choose to spend instead of saving and investing. We craft an image based on what we think will make others envious instead of building real wealth.

We rest when we should work. We cheat on our spouses and our diets, miss workouts, accept handouts, choose TV over reading, and so on. We consistently choose to move away from our biggest goals and toward a life of failure, weakness and dependency. Again, we do this by choice, though the effects of said choices aren't fully realized until years later.

**We actively *choose* momentary pleasure over wealth, success, and happiness.** But we do so incrementally, not giving these seemingly insignificant daily, even hourly choices that we make incorrectly, the weight they deserve. Slowly we become the opposite of who we want to be.

Too many people think that they're a victim to their circumstances. They wake up one day and realize that they're failing, that the path they're heading down isn't a good one. It hits them like a ton of bricks. I've been there. I've felt that. I felt sorry for myself. I pitied my situation and wanted out of it.

I had to step back, detach, and see what got me there, and it was a year of daily bad decision-making. That's it. It starts with bending to a desire in the moment once, like a missed workout, which gives you reason to miss another, and then another. And then you're weak and fat.

For me, it was undisciplined spending that got in the way of building the business initially. The problem was solved by both lowering my bottom line through discipline, and increasing my top line through discipline. A lack of focus stalled growth and its opposite enabled growth.

The undisciplined spending happened very early in the business, but it took time for me to see the negative effect it was having. When I changed and got my act together, the results, again, took time to show themselves.

Momentum takes time. You have to feed it daily, even

methodically and persistently to see it create something grand. But it takes time in the negative sense, too. If you consistently make poor decisions you will eventually see their result down the road where you realize you are not where you had intended to go.

## Your Perfect Morning

Discipline is won or lost early. The battle begins when the alarm rings and the best thing you can do is make as *few* decisions as humanly possible.

There's a reason behind Steve Jobs' eventual singular wardrobe; it was to remove an unnecessary decision from his day. Who needs to spend time thinking about what they're going to wear when that mental energy *could be spent* on something much more important, or important in general. If anything, your wardrobe - if it's something that needs to be chosen at all - should be decided upon the night before, *never* the day of. When the day begins, limiting the unnecessary decision-making in your life on things like your first meal, your second meal, your clothing and so forth, gives you more mental energy to tackle the things that are actually important, like a business-decision or even what word to choose to write on a page like this one.

Thus, a morning must have a plan, a habitual routine that can be completed without thought and without having to make even a single decision.

I rise, do push-ups, put on jeans and a shirt, have a big glass of water, a double espresso, read a book, and then start writing.

Life can be very chaotic. We cannot predict or control much of what happens in our lives and in the world. We can, however, far more often than not, predict and control and plan the first hour of our day. The habit of waking up and letting life *happen* cannot continue if our goal is to succeed.

# Wake up an hour before you have to

This becomes even more important when you have a family that needs things from you even if that thing is attention. You have to rise before that first little one does, before your lady does, heck, before the pup does. Start your day by enacting some semblance of control and in the rarity that is silence before the rugrats run rampant.

This isn't a difficult thing to do. All it entails is that you also go to be an hour earlier. It really is simple, but the effect on your life can be incredible. A day should not be rushed, discipline doesn't have room for busyness. Getting up earlier gives you time to live at a purposeful pace before everyone else in your house or in your life or in your business tries to take your time and attention to help their day or even to just feel like they're doing something.

There's also the aforementioned issue of silence. It can be incredibly rare, and we need more of it in our lives. Creating time in the morning that's silent helps us focus on what's important rather than on everything.

# Make your bed

Accomplish something early. Make your bed. This sets the stage for your day. You feel like a winner before you leave your bedroom. It gives you the sense of self-reliance and responsibility you need to win the day. There's so much we can't control, so begin the day by taking action on something you can control and spend the rest of the day carrying on that momentum. Jordan Peterson talks about this a lot. His view is a great one. *How can you go out and change the world if you don't even have your own room in order?*

We have to start from a place of strength. That place of

strength is our cave, our castle, an area that must be in order if we're going to do something of value outside of it.

## Read and write

Learn and clarify. Reading offers another perspective that you weren't exposed to before you opened the book. Quite simply, it makes you a smarter human. Never go anywhere without a book in hand or on your tablet or however you consume the thing. Starting your day with reading puts something into your subconscious, a problem, an idea, that your brain mulls over the rest of the day.

Journaling first thing in the morning provides clarity. It gives focus to your effort and energy and can, as in my case, dramatically improve your discipline.

Putting both at the beginning of your day cannot help but help you improve. The goal, after-all, is to be better today than we were yesterday. Reading helps you do that, and journaling ensures that you will succeed in said quest. With your journal you can *see* your improvement or failure and work on ensuring that you only see improvement.

## Accept pain as good

So soft we have become that we can spend an entire week, day, month and so on, without feeling pain, and it won't necessarily mean our failure. A life with no pain, however, is one where we're going to get softer, weaker, and fatter. Over time, we'll see how a lack of pain has made us weak, but it can take a while, and it can take even longer to once again see the positive results that come from physical pain.

Pain inflicted on the body through exercise of some kind isn't just an exercise to toughen the body, but a necessary exercise to toughen the mind. Soft people don't succeed, especially when they're pitted against tough people.

Do something active, feel some pain first thing in the morning to wake up your nervous system and get your blood pumping. Start with push-ups or pull-ups. Throw in a cold shower. Both have a similar effect and both are highly recommended.

When you get your blood flowing early and stimulate your nerves, you'll need to rely less on things like caffeine to keep you awake and focused later in the morning. Pain, moreover, is good. Add pain to your life in the way of push-ups and a cold shower, and you're accepting the uncomfortable, which is what self-improvement requires.

You cannot improve amid comfort. That's not how it works. Improvement is necessarily painful and uncomfortable. Including physical pain in the morning trains your brain to accept rather than avoid it the way most of society does.

The other side of pain is that it's required to develop toughness. No good has come from being anyone being soft, being a pussy (look up pusillanimous if you get your panties in a knot about the use of such a word). Toughness and grit were once necessary qualities for survival, and are now necessary qualities for one to live a flourishing life, for one to improve, to succeed, to avoid giving up.

Do things that you don't feel like doing. Do them early. And you will avoid the weakness and laziness that can claim a day, then a week, and then a life.

## Your Perfect Evening

They saying goes, *win your morning, win your day.* To extend that, if you win your day, and you win enough of them, you win your life. In my humble experience, however, my morning is dependent on how I *ended* the previous day as much as it is about my morning habits.

I've learned by reading the words of smarter men than I, like Cal Newport who wrote *Deep Work*, that the end of a work day should be firm, not simply 'when the work is finished', which is what I always used to do. As a result of having your work day end 'when the work is finished', you don't give yourself the power of a deadline, nor do you give yourself the time to plan the next day to ensure that *it, too*, is won.

What comes first, the chicken or the egg, the morning or the evening?

Again, in my experience, the evening comes before the morning because it's when you both grade your day, plan your next, and ensure that you stay the course.

It's also far more effective to plan after having just completed work rather than planning at the start of a new day when options are endless and opportunities seem limitless. I read somewhere that Hemingway wouldn't completely finish a thought by day's end, instead leaving that thought open so as to be able to jumping back into something that has momentum rather than having to start anew. Planning your day after having just finished work (or just having finished a work period) means that you can prepare tomorrow to begin with momentum rather than having to wake up and think about *plans* rather than actions.

Thus, the evening demands just as much, if not more, respect and reverence than the morning receives.

Discipline isn't just related to hardcore work or training. It's not just about masochistically doing the yard work or undertaking only life's arduous and unpleasant tasks. Discipline also relates to freedom and joy.

In fact, discipline *promotes* freedom and joy. It frees you from having to look at your watch and allows you to take joy in being in the present doing what you want to do with the people you want to do it with. It gives you the peace that comes from having done your work, and done it well. If you're ambitious, you always feel like you need to do more, I get that. There can be nervousness, worry attached to your work life. Discipline removes this stress while helping you accomplish more and enjoying life outside of work and within work to a far greater degree.

To have freedom, you need discipline.

Without discipline, you are not free, you're lost, trying to be found or to find what will help you become found.

Any ambitious human will feel guilty about not getting work done. I do. I hate it. I don't feel at peace if I know there's a list of unfinished tasks awaiting my attention and if I go off track or lack discipline or get stuck in busy mode that stress is with me by day's end.

Discipline ensures that you don't feel that stress. To be honest it's not the discipline of the action, the doing of the task, that's easy, you just do it. You shut your brain off and do what you've laid out for yourself. It's the planning that helps me avoid the vice-like stress at a day's end where little was accomplished.

It takes discipline to stay the course both in the run of a day and in the course of a lifetime. But the planning of said course is easily as important. When I fail to plan, I fail. When I plan, and don't let my brain come up with a better idea, I win.

What's lost in speech about discipline is the day's end, when what has happened up to that point is reflected on, and what must happen tomorrow is identified. Rarely do we read or hear about how a prominent CEO or artist ends the day or why that end of day sets them up for a better next day. Perhaps we assume they live days without end.

The end is the beginning, but it's also a necessary finality, a deadline.

Your day needs a defining end for the same reason your goals require six-month deadlines: **urgency**. Without urgency, we lag in our habits, we procrastinate. Ensuring a firm end to my day has improved the quality of my work, the quantity of my work, and the quality of my life. It will be as powerful an addition to your day as your morning habits, if not a more powerful one. The urgency imposed on you when you set a firm, earlier-than-wanted end to your day helps you in three main areas:

1.  **It forces you to focus during the day**

When there is no end to the day, the day never ends. This usually means that the work you need to get done at the beginning of the day and throughout the day never gets done because there's always later. It's when there isn't a later and only a finite end to the day that you're forced to complete what you're supposed to complete.

2.  **It allows more thinking time**

The other day I had a conversation with my lady about technology. Earlier that day, while she was at work, she decided to go for a walk during her lunch break, but instead of texting me as she typically does on breaks, she explored. She loved it. There was so much in her work area that she didn't realize was there. The break truly acted as a break, refreshing her mind so she could go back to work and work well.

Every day after work she hops on the train to head home. There aren't conversations, there are only eyes fixated on screens. *People aren't living*, she said, and I agreed. It's a sentiment shared by many. Much of the pleasure and peace we get from life comes from simple things that make us happy and appreciative, yet, we rob ourselves of such things by engaging primarily in a world that is virtual and not real.

By being lost in the screen on our phone we rob ourselves of the quiet time that enabled us to solve problems, to find clarity, and to think. Today, we're forever distracted and rarely bored. Disconnect from headphones and screens to work a farm field, ride a horse, walk, run, row a boat, drive your vehicle, cut your lawn, whatever, and you'll soon be forced to think out of boredom if nothing else.

We live in the worst and the best of times for discipline. Our many distracting options make discipline tough. We're on our phones, listening to tunes, or viewing things on our computers or tablets. We're seldom free to truly think, especially if you have a business like mine, where you can work all day and check the various apps on your phone that gauge success.

This is why it's never been more important to be disciplined, disciplined enough to put a firm cap to the day and to unplug from distractions. As you unwind at day's end, you'll find yourself thinking about and enjoying life. You'll solve problems in your work and family life. You'll find the peace that's all but lost in a society and a culture that avoids silence, solitude, and peace at all costs.

### 3.   It helps you sleep

The insomnia I suffered from for a large part of my life left my mind racing at times I most needed it to be silent. A firm sleep schedule and shutting down my day firmly at 6 p.m., with no more time on the phone or computer, has dramatically improved the quality of my sleep.

## How to Create the Perfect Evening

### Set your firm end time

You must determine when you're going to shut down your work. Make it a rule, not a suggestion.

### Proclaim its end

In his book *Deep Work*, Cal Newport talks about the necessity of proclaiming an end to the workday rather than allowing it to happen organically. *I'm done!* or *Finito!* provide the trigger words for your brain to shut down. It sounds corny, but it works. Your post work day cannot have work dominating your mind.

Personally, I need to use the harshest word possible to hammer home this idea of an end. *Fuckin' done!* Work over. Post work day begins.

### Write down a problem

Before you proclaim the end of your work day, write down a problem in your life or your business that you want to solve, then don't think about it. Let your subconscious do its work overnight. This may sound hokey, but try it. Upon waking, a resolution to the problem may well present itself. Keep a pen and pad by your bedside on which to record the solution.

Business, entrepreneurship, writing, and life in general, all involve problem-solving. If you can solve a problem that afflicts a lot of people that no one else has solved, you have the potential to make a lot of money. Sometimes, however, our thoughts can cloud the solution, and getting our brain out of the way can be the necessary action we need to take. You'll likely know this, but maybe you haven't put it into practice, but solutions to life's biggest problems can often come when we're not focused on the issue we're trying to solve.

Write it down, and leave it. Let your unconscious brain take over.

## How to Plan Your Perfect Evening

While your day, the things you have to accomplish, demand a plan, your evening requires space, freedom, and a few habits. There are things we can do in our evening that will help us live better, more productive and efficient lives. Here are a couple of the things I've implemented into my evenings that have helped me a lot. They're simple, small habits that yield big results and provide much needed clarity.

### Write down ten ideas

At the end of the work day, try this. It doesn't matter how horrible they are, write down ten ideas to get you thinking like a problem-solver. Too often we're focused on problems, and not ideas. Problems are great because they're things we can solve in our lives, but what about ideas? What about growth? What about things that excite us? We too often brush them off, but thinking in terms of ideas keeps your mind open and focused on new ideas not past failures.

**Express gratitude for three things from
the past twenty-four hours**

Indicating gratitude is the most important of my end-of-day evening habits. It's something I really have had to work on implementing. To be honest, I thought it was a hokey activity. I thought it was new age nonsense so I didn't give it the respect it deserves - and it's a habit that deserves not only respect, but reverence.

I'm an ambitious fella, like yourself, and as ambitious fellas we tend to think about how we need to improve, what we want in our lives, and where we want to go, but rarely do we sit and appreciate what we already have, what we've done, and who we have in our lives.

Man, is it ever powerful.

It can take the stress and worry and anxiety in your day and completely flush it from your mind.

Being thankful for three things within the past twenty-four hours is an idea I got from Craig Ballantyne, the author of the great book *The Perfect Day Formula*. A commitment to expressing gratitude dovetails nicely with discipline.

We all need to be more disciplined in how we view our lives. It's easy to be blind to the good in them and cynical amid endless bad news and constant comparison. Small things especially can be overlooked in the run of a day. But discipline yourself to express gratitude for three things daily, and your life will improve immeasurably.

It takes time to sit and think about these 3 things, but it's time well spent. Sometimes I'll do this while I walk or run, but switching your mindframe from one of fear - we're bombarded with news and images and ideas that make us see things in a fearful light - to one of gratitude is a powerful switch. No matter where you are in life or how life is going, there are things to be grateful for. There are always things to be grateful for, we just have to once again train our minds to focus on the good, the blessings, rather than constantly focusing on the curses that are often blessings in disguise.

# The Necessary Acquisition of Grit

*Grit is sticking with your future day in,*
*day out and not just for the week, not*
*just for the month, but for years.*

—*Angela Lee Duckworth*

Discipline without toughness is useless. Toughness, or grit, is what enables you to persist.

Without grit, you're soft. If you're soft, you cannot accomplish anything. And softness has invaded our society, which means that if you're to acquire grit, you have to do it purposefully, with intention, not merely by allowing life to present it to you.

As a man, softness means you cannot lead. Softness means you won't protect or provide. Softness makes a man useless, literally and figuratively impotent.

Grit is simply discipline over the long run. It's persistence. It's pushing through or around setbacks and obstacles without giving up.

Grit is necessary. It's endurance to see not only your mission in life through, but to see a well-lived life to its culmination. Forget about the project you're working on and commit to living *life* well, to improving daily, to living how you'd like to live every day. It has to become who you are not just what you do from time to time.

Maybe you've had an intense dream that you allowed to fizzle out when success didn't arrive. Sometimes it's simply not the right dream. Other times, we don't give the dream the effort and time needed for its realization. I've had many dreams come and go and, to be frank, they didn't always go because they were the wrong dream. They went because I felt entitled to success, and when it didn't come I thought it was the goal that was wrong, when it was my mindset that needed to change.

Discipline isn't just something we need in the present, it has to apply to how we pursue everything in life, including how long we pursue things. Practice staying the course. Practice grit.

## The Devil is in TOMORROW
### Overcoming procrastination

*You may delay, but time will not, and*
*lost time is never found again.*

*~ Benjamin Franklin*

What is to be done today, must be done today. There's a myth that tomorrow exists and that it's just as viable a time to do something as is today. So as we halt, stop, or even regress, time doesn't. It constantly moves forward, so to match it, we must do the same.

Procrastination is laziness. It's enabled by listening to opinions in one's own mind about what should be done rather than doing what that same mind had already decided to do.

How do you stop procrastinating?

You stop procrastinating.

In the intro of this book I talked briefly about the mindlessness of action, of how boxing and business helped me shut my brain off and just do, rather than thinking about *what to do*. If you've paid attention to this book you'll likely have already set your planning time. This is when you think. This is when you determine correct action. With the choice having already been made, there is no decision when it comes time to act.

What you have set out to do is what you do. Nothing gets in its way because there's nothing else you set out to get done. TV doesn't stand between you and the book you want to write. Tiredness isn't a barrier that prevents you from working out. Tomorrow isn't when you planned to do what you have on your to do list, today is.

Time keeps moving. Pushing things to tomorrow is a horrible habit to form and a very effective habit to break.

If you genuinely want to become better, stronger, tougher, and more FREE, breaking this habit of procrastination is so necessary it's hard to overstate. To stop procrastination you depend on a few things we've covered in this book:

1. You need to plan tomorrow at the end of today. Don't wait to the day of to plan what must be done.

2. You need to start small, really small. Have one vital task that must be completed and for the first couple of weeks of your quest to defeat procrastination, accomplish this single thing and keep it to a single thing. This is your foundation, this one thing. Every morning you're going to do it, and you're not going to think about whether or not you have to do it.

3. You need to set parameters. I'm writing this in a cafe that has no internet - parameter number one. I have my cell phone on silent, parameter number two, with a timer set to 45-minutes for this writing block, parameter number three. Nothing but work on this book is done while that timer is on. When it rings, I close up, pay the bill, and leave.

These rules make this task's accomplishment inevitable, and I need these rules or else I'll actively avoid the work that must be done. I chose this task because I believe that it, along with a few other things, will make the success of this mission I'm on inevitable as well. Without this 45 minute writing block, if I were to push it to tomorrow, it becomes less inevitable, and if I procrastinate often enough, *failure becomes inevitable.*

Discipline takes the uncertainty of achievement and makes it dramatically more certain. It's uncertainty that prevents many from adopting self-discipline, which does create more certainty, just not for the things they think they want.

## Iron Sharpening Iron
### How to make something habitual

To confine discipline to a single area of your life is to practice *not being disciplined* in every other area of your life. What you practice outside of your single focus will eventually invade that area.

**When you're starting a workout program,
aim to train once a week.**

If you presently train once a month, don't launch full bore into a new program, which for most programs means a four-day split. Just get in the habit of doing something because something is better than nothing.

Begin training once a week for a month. Thereafter, add a workout to your training week. Gradually build to the full four-day-a-week program. This ensures that you'll be ready for four days of training. It shouldn't be an incredible shock to your system. It should, however, be followed without breaks.

I lift weights every second day like clockwork. I've done 4 day splits and 6 day splits and they're nice, but I train not to look better in the mirror, but to be able to do more with my life and to become tougher. Training every second day is something I can maintain for the rest of my life. It's more routine to me than is training 4 days in a week and then taking 3 days off or 5 days a week and then taking 2 days off.

Those days off are active. I go running, hiking, shooting, fishing, mountain-biking. I do something that my training has allowed me to do.

I *need* the every-second day method because of its rhythm. So no matter the split, I train every second day.

**Use pain to discipline yourself to develop habits of toughness.**

The gym is a wonderful place to become tougher if we're aware of our mental battles during workouts. Take it a step further.

You're after more than mediocrity. Who you are every day determines what you will become and accomplish. Add more discipline and thus more discomfort to your life, and you become tougher. The more pain you face with a smile, the tougher you become.

## Do push-ups every morning

Exercising first thing in the day is on the list of nearly every contemporary high performer I've come across. Even if you already work out in the morning, start your day with push-ups. It can be as few as one push-up, just do push-ups and whatever number you can do consistently. Add this to your perfect morning.

## Run

Long-form cardio runs have fallen into disrepute in recent years because they're not the most efficient way to burn fat. I'm not arguing. They are, however, a great way to get tougher.

Run not to get ripped or shredded but because there are

moments within every run when you'll want to quit. It's at these moments when we choose our fate. They're that important. The more of these moments we have, the tougher we're going to be, if we make the right choice, the tough choice.

Navy SEALs run. Any special operations unit runs. Running is a mental test and a skill we'll need at some point in our lives if we want a life where things get a little hairy at times.

Train in whatever fashion you'd like. Just add these two habits of push-ups and runs to your life daily.

## You Are What You Read and Watch

At the end of this book is a reading list. It includes *Essentialism*, a Stoic- themed book for determining what should command your attention.

We've talked about identifying what deserves our attention in this book already, but it's something that bears repeat consideration. What you watch and read has profound implications for all areas of your life.

If you read crap tabloids and magazines that venerate image over substance, you're leading your brain away in a direction opposed to the life you ideally want to lead. If you watch crap TV shows filled with petty nonsense, you're shaping your mind for little things.

Read *Essentialism*. Study the Stoics. Heed what you're paying attention to.

*Note: I've begun far too many books that just weren't worth completing, at the time at least. Now, before I read or buy a book I check out blinkist.com - a website that gives good, detailed book reviews so as to help readers avoid buying and reading things that aren't worth their time. I get nothing from sharing this link, it's just been a wonderful tool that was passed on to me by a friend.*

**Discern what deserves your attention.**

You're trying to form new and better habits and to break old and bad ones in every aspect of your life. Specify what you want to watch on TV and why. Is it for escape, for winding down at the end of the day (a book is better and avoids the blue-light glimmer of a TV screen), or for education.

There is value in TV. It can provide a window into different ways of life. You can "watch" good writing. You can learn from shows. You can see how the rest of the world lives and gain inspiration to travel. You can get the news, but be careful. The news is on the list of crap. It's more subjective views than objective news. And it shines a negative light on parts of the world that, when you travel there, are nothing like how they've been portrayed.

Be discerning in what you watch and read. From the mindset of studying to be better than you are now, select shows and written materials that open and improve your mind, that guide you in the right direction, that educate you on how the world is and how it may one day be.

**Be purposeful.**

The disciplined life is lived on purpose, with purpose.

You're not living at the behest of the media or your friends or your folks or your teachers. You're living on your terms, with a clarity that demands you ask if what you're doing is worth your time. It requires that you have the discipline to discern whether or not you're being pulled in the wrong direction.

Most people give into someone else's idea for their life. They do it unknowingly by adhering to someone else's expectations for what they should do with their lives. Maybe they see college as something they must do, without giving thought to why or even to what they should take. Maybe they enter a profession because their old man was in it.

The point is, many of us do things without intent or purpose. We wake up without reason or thought. We watch and read and buy without determining if any of it aligns with our goal, if we've even set a goal.

You have to have a plan, a direction, a code that guides you, or else you're like seaweed, tossed by the ocean. Be purposeful in how you live. Have a clear goal and structure everything you do to bring you closer to that goal.

**Measure everything.**

The difference between success and failure is often a matter of knowing what's working and what isn't, knowing if you're winning or losing; metrics.

In his book *Good to Great*, Jim Collins discusses the similarities among some of the most successful companies of the past few decades.

If you don't know where you are or specifically how you're doing with the habits you're trying to create, any expectation on your part that they'll develop by chance is unrealistic, as that's unlikely.

This applies to business, where you have to track everything, growth, costs and so forth. It applies to your workouts, where you *need* to track your progress, how much weight you're lifting and for how many reps so you can see your improvement. Why would you not track progress in life, in who you are day in and day out? Whatever you or I want in this life is dependent on us, thus, our improvement should be taken pretty damn seriously.

You are your habits. Whether you're successful or not is essentially a matter of being efficient or inefficient. Track your efficiency. There are a myriad of ways to do it, but until focus becomes your way of living, documenting your behavior is incredibly powerful. When I began to track what I was doing it was like a slap in the face. I was not acting like I knew I could act. I was underperforming by a large margin, and *seeing it* woke me up to that reality.

If we don't see it in an app or on paper, we usually go about our day as we usually would, inefficiently.

Measuring habits, of course, calls for tracking systems different than for other things. For tracking habits, I've found the Way of Life app to be of value. It's in the iTunes app store. I'm sure it's available for other phones as well as the iPhone. It's a tracking system that reminds you when a habit should occur and that asks you if you've done it or not.

This is good accountability. You can measure your progress and see if you're forging the discipline and creating a habit. But an better system for tracking habit development is that of Ben Franklin. You list the virtues, or habits, that you want to live by, and you check off any you've adhered to at every day's end.

Throughout the book I've mentioned that the most important form of discipline is *self-discipline,* as it's the only form that benefits you and I, the individual trying to become better. You are the man looking over your shoulder. You don't lie to yourself if you have any ounce of ambition and self-respect or honesty. If you can hold yourself accountable, there's no need for coaches or mentors or bosses or managers in your life.

That's how it should be, too. Which is why having a tracking system for your habits is important. You form a true relationship with yourself. You're honest with yourself, where you're at and what you have to do to get to where you want to be. When you're truthful with yourself, when you don't make excuses or try to rationalize your failure to adhere to something, you develop a solid foundation, a personality founded on honor, self-respect, and truth.

Most people don't have that. They make excuses for themselves (which are either pure lies or a distorted perspective), and thus, lie to others. They're worms, without the skeleton that makes men stand erec - not the bones in our body, but the honor in which we carry ourselves.

Track your progress. Tell the truth. And don't depend on someone else to ensure you're following through on what you said you'd do. Hold *yourself* accountable. Act like a man in that sense. Don't be a dependent.

## Your Journal

I've found journals to be very helpful for a number of reasons. One journal I use - called the *Effic Journal,* found at *effic.co* - is specifically used to help you achieve what you want to achieve, to stay the course and to not deviate when something newer and more exciting crosses my desk.

That journal helps you define your ideal, your goals within the year, break them down to quarterly achievements that have to be met to reach the ideal goals, and then weekly and daily tasks that have to be completed to have a successful quarter.

I *depend* on that journal. It takes the macro and helps you focus on the micro, the things you can control and must complete to create your overarching ideal.

If you want to use the practices in this book, the *Effic* journal, created by my pal Dave Ruel, is a wonderful addition to your life. It helps you make sure that your daily tasks align with your overall mission, ideal, and quest.

The second journal is purely for thoughts and ideas.

Keep it by your bed at night, and near your desk during the day.

These journals help us focus and stay the course. The ideas journal isn't just about work. I write my thoughts in that one because keeping them as thoughts isn't always enough, they get lost in a sea of other thoughts and writing them down helps them become goals, intentions, and ideas that can be acted on later.

**Clarity is found by writing things down.**

We can't simply think. We must document. That's the purpose of journals. They're there for clarity, for solving problems, and for recording and keeping a tab on the habits that we've discussed in this book.

They're also used for reflection.

Who I am now is who I once wanted to be - maybe not completely, but close.

I once wanted to earn what I now earn, live in a house like I now live in - okay, I've always wanted land and lot's of it, but this house is awesome, it's something that I never thought would be mine, especially when I was 3 years into running my own business and still not seeing any growth. I have a great lady who's intelligent, funny, supportive, and beautiful. I have a pup that I love, a routine that helps me win, and because I'm ambitious, I rarely appreciate what I have or where I am or who surrounds me.

Without past journals and the ability to go back on reflect where I was two, three, five, and even ten years ago, my appreciation for where I am wouldn't have the context I need to *truly* feel proud - in a good sense - about where I am.

I have so bloody far to go, as do you. That will be true for your entire life. You're always going to be wanting more. You're always going to take a step backward. You're going to do things you're not proud of, but if you treat each day as its own, if you act in a consistent manner, creating the right habits in your life, in a year's time, five year's time, in a few decades, you're going to be proud of what you've done, the man you are, and what you've earned.

Keep writing. Don't throw these journals out. They're worth more than gold. They give you something that few ever take the time to have, clarity and perspective.

Get after it.

# Daring Discipline

## Discipline Becomes Effortless

There will be a point, usually around the 80-day mark, where your habit becomes, well, a habitual. They become innate. Just like your present habit of checking Facebook or emails or sleeping in, your NEW habit will eventually become, simply put, what you do and a part of who you are.

Discipline, initially, requires willpower and effort. Eventually it is who you are and how you act. Though the battle will always exist, it will get easier. It becomes something more than an intention but a being, a way of life, a standard that you hold yourself to. You get to the point where you don't really have to think all that much about doing something you've set out to do, you just do it, and then you do the next thing you've planned on doing.

That's the silver lining. It is what you should aspire to create. When you discover what you really want in life and create the habits and disciplines around this ideal end game, and you work toward the end game every day and you eventually *become* your habits, your disciplines, this man you once deemed it impossible to be, you end up living a life that's genuinely on your terms, which is incredibly refreshing and rare.

When you want to accomplish something, you accomplish it. When you want to save for something, you save for it. When you want to do something, you move the pieces of the puzzle that is your life around to accommodate this adventure you're intent on embarking upon.

## Discipline is freedom.

While we've talked at length about habit-forming and how to create disciplines in your life, you have to remember why you're doing this.

I get lost in my work, which is good, but bad as well. It's been a month, essentially, where I've gone without doing what I love to do. I love hiking, hunting, exploring. I love bringing my rifle to a field, setting up a target, and practicing. I love the outdoors, but I've been working me arse off trying to finish multiple projects because my discipline lagged in the months prior (with that said, I went hunting in Africa, so that should have quenched those desires for a time).

A few months prior to finishing this book I regressed. I stopped using work blocks every day, I got away from using the timer on the work blocks and tackling a few important things in the run of the day rather than trying to do everything at once.

I found myself stressed and ineffective. Editing this book for a final time provided a jolt back to the best way of doing things, the best way of living.

You're going to have periods where you regress, where you slowly slip back into bad habits. They're irrelevant. Recognize them, then snap back into the way of life described in these pages. You'll remove stress and worry, and replace it with accomplishment, peace, and freedom.

Discipline is the stress-killer. It's the liberator. It's the path of least resistance, oddly enough, because initially the resistance is plenty.

Clarity is king when it comes to living a more disciplined life. Knowing what you really want versus what you think you want or what you're told you want or what a clever native ad insinuates that you should want is a necessity. People can be disciplined on the wrong things and lack discipline on the things that, if they were disciplined, they'd have more money, more time, more freedom, more meaning, more purpose, and more happiness.

While you've gone through these pages quickly, I'm sure, take time to reflect on this ideal you developed in the early pages of the book. Is it what you really want?

If it is, start dissecting down from the ideal, way down to the habits that this goal requires, even to the thoughts that you should think, the desires and feelings you should focus on and pursue, and those you shouldn't. Set time aside to plan, and once the plan is set, do, do not spend too much time thinking. **If a thought stands between you and the action you have to take, remove the thought.**

No dream that you set out to achieve should ask that you be envious. You shouldn't look at your neighbor and want what he has. You shouldn't envy the life he lives or the truck he drives. You shouldn't fantasize about what others have. It does you no good. It turns you into an envious, cynical human which the world has far too many of.

Focus on your own journey, your own pursuits, and remember the perfect day you created, the one you can live today.

I forget this far too often, the perfect day with what I already have and who I already am.

For too long I solely set my sights on how I ultimately wanted my life to be. I dreamt of the ranch, the land, the coffee in the morning on the wrap around porch and the horseback ride with the lady on my first work break. I put myself in the mindframe that I needed these *things* to have the peace I craved, the accomplishment I desired. When I changed my focus from being dependent on things I do not yet have, to what I have now, I was able to create the structure, the productivity, and the gratitude that we need to perform at our best.

What I found, too, is that the day is essentially the same, and that when it's lived, I produce more, I live more, I have more freedom and far less stress, and these grand future goals are brought closer, faster.

When you aim high and then create the structure that allows you to focus on the steps you need to take rather than the summit that's hours away, you're then tasked with remaining present, in the work rather than in a time and place that does not exist, and will not exist if you do not work efficiently, live efficiently and daringly.

The solution to the wandering mind is too simple that we often don't want to hear it; **you don't allow thoughts that don't belong to breathe.**

You know what thoughts are worthy of your attention, and which take you away from the work that you have to do.

When I have a day that I don't perform well, where distractions win and I try to do a bunch of things that aren't on my to do list, I'm stressed and worried and I work longer hours but get less good work done. My perfect day goes at a slow, deliberate pace where one task is tackled after another, never multiple tasks achieved at the same time.

When you appreciate where you are or even simply appreciate what you're able to work on or who you're with or the challenge you're facing, the stress of where you want to be is alleviated. It isn't that stress is a bad thing; we need it. We need productive paranoia to keep us striving and improving, but the pace that stress can thrust us into can become incredibly *unproductive*. The stress of improvement is required. The stress of worry is not. **The wrong kind of stress can move you from being productive to being busy.** All you care about is getting done what must be completed. If you can do it at a high quality, in less time, do it, don't become busy just because you feel that being busy means being a winner, because it doesn't, and your ideal day should reflect that. You need time to think, time to live, time to have fun and unwind, and you can have that time while getting more work done.

**You already have the capacity to become who you want to be, who your grand goals need you to become.** Start living *his life*. That is, don't wait for a promotion, for more money to come rolling in, for that house you want or the land you want that house to be on, **be that man, now, have his habits, his confidence, his assertiveness and discipline, and the *things* that make up your future ideal will come.**

These words are assertions that I have to hammer home to myself, daily. In the morning I can shut off and work, but as the day goes and my mind tries to wander or a picture of what could be my ideal house or a hunting trip I'd love to go on crosses my eyes, the danger of being elsewhere is real. This future desire we have, this goal or dream or ideal, is necessary for guidance, to have a direction to point our lives to is a must, but to spend too much time thinking about that place can make you make the wrong moves.

You think you have to do something grand, now, and the persistent, methodical work you're doing just doesn't seem like it's enough, but it is, it always is.

Catching yourself in that moment is paramount, where you pull yourself back from the dream and into the reality that is the present, the work that must get done, the fun and joy and pain and victory that can be had in the here and now.

Forget about that end for a second and focus only on being the man that can earn that end in the present. That's your task, nay, your duty as a man, a leader, a warrior. You have to become who you can become as soon as possible and to waste any more time not being him is pushing that achievement you crave further into the future.

*Why wait to get something you don't yet have to validate this character, discipline, persona, charisma, and courage? Why not be him, then let the validation come, even if said validation takes a decade to arrive?*

Of course we're on a journey, one wrought with unexpected turns and failures and triumphs, but much of what we want can already be had. Much of who we're trying to become can already be lived.

Find clarity. Search hard for it. Determine exactly both the man and what that man creates every day. **Become the man *now*, and let what he creates evolve as a natural creation of the habits you develop and the discipline you incur.**

Know where you want to be and who you want to be, and sprinkle an abundance of audacity on that dream. Multiply it tenfold. Make it something you're excited to pursue and willing to sacrifice it all to gain. This vision is what will help you become the man you need to become. Make it grand.

### Be Dangerous

*For believe me! — the secret for harvesting from existence the greatest fruitfulness and the greatest enjoyment is: to live dangerously! Build your cities on the slopes of Vesuvius! Send your ships into uncharted*

*seas! Live at war with your peers and yourselves!*
*Be robbers and conquerors as long as you cannot be*
*rulers and possessors, you seekers of knowledge! Soon*
*the age will be past when you could be content to*
*live hidden in forests like shy deer! At long last the*
*search for knowledge will reach out for its due: — it*
*will want to rule and possess, and you with it!*

~*Friedrich Nietzsche*

To find danger and the excitement of adventure, you have to take risks. It doesn't mean stupidity or ignorance, but taking the necessary actions that your goal require. That's risk. It's time and effort, it's danger and audacity, it's facing fears and going against the grain. It may mean debt and despair that you're alone with, that no one around you can really relate to. They don't understand why you're aiming so high, why you're working so hard, why you're doing something that doesn't seem to be working. I've been there.

I've been working long hours at a business that had yet to bear fruit. Everyone wanted me to quit out of kindness and caring, but you can't. You have to pivot and adjust course from time to time but the direction you're heading in and the effort you're giving is consistent, it has to be consistent.

While we've talked at length about being disciplined, too many equate that with being safe, with confining yourself to a set of rules and principles, never accepting that daring, audacity, and living dangerously have to be a part of those principles.

Discipline gives you the freedom to pursue danger with courage, and with the abilities you need to be successful with your dangerous endeavor.

There is no more safety. There cannot be any ounce of mediocrity in what you aspire to achieve and conquer any longer.

Dare mightily. Live dangerously. And do each, successful, with discipline.

*"A fight isn't a fight until there's*
*something to overcome."*

**Teddy Atlas**

The book was written, edited, and ready for print. And then I listened to Joe Rogan and Teddy Atlas talk. I've read Teddy Atlas' book, if you don't know who he is, he's a great trainer, the former trainer of heavyweight champion Michael Moorer and one of Mike Tyson's original trainers when he was a young, powerful buck.

The quote above is applicable to the end of this book where we've talked about persistence and consistency, discipline and focus, and where we live in a world or a society that is getting soft. We're more entitled than ever before and we've discussed some of the reasons for this, including the fact that we can compare a perception of someone else's life with ours without having to talk to them or get to know them, but simply by viewing the images they choose to publish online.

We've also talked about how we have to stay in our lane.

But, who are you? And how do you *know* who you are?

You don't actually know you're who you think you are until you face resistance.

In the podcast with Joe Rogan, Atlas talks about Mike Tyson and his place in history amount the all-time greats in boxing. *Tyson is 0 and 5*, Atlas says after some explanation. The logic is that there were 5 times where Tyson faced adversity, where he was actually in a fight, partially because of his incredible talent, there were only 5 occasions (to clarify, he wasn't certain of Tyson's actual record). When he faced someone who didn't care about his aura, who pushed back when he fought, he lost.

That's when Atlas provides us with the gem above, *A fight isn't a fight until there's some resistance*, just like *life isn't life until there's some resistance*, without resistance it's just existence, it isn't living.

Discipline is as much an aid to help you get to where you want to go as it is training to be able to endure the resistance in life with will inevitably present itself, and that you should *want* to experience. It's in tribulation that you find out what you're made of, and you better not carry entitlement or weakness or softness into the battle because you will be exposed.

Know that there is no way out of the battle. There is only accountability. There is only fighting back. You won't bite the ear of an opponent to find a way out of the struggle, you'll dig deep and land a harder counter. You'll take a step forward into the fire and *show* the struggle that you're formidable, that you won't be broken, you will find a way to win.

Prepare yourself for this inevitable difficulty that life thrusts into our lap at the seemingly worst time by waking up early, doing your push ups, running and training, lifting and suffering when you do not need to suffer at all. When life can be easy, find ways to incorporate pain. Find ways to bring more discomfort into your life because when the option for ease is gone, that training, that discipline is what you'll fall back on.

Tough times are merely a part of life. Your problems are not unique. You are not the only one going through what you're going through, in fact, there are more people going through far worse. Put your head down and get through it, with discipline as your greatest weapon.

## READING LIST

There are *many* books that are valuable in helping you further both your understanding of discipline, and the skills and attributes that will help you actually be able to embody what discipline is - like toughness, grit, and persistence.

What follows is a shortlist of books you should own if you'd like to become a more disciplined human. Each are practical, helpful, and will simply help you become both a better man and a more successful human, though they're not the typical self-help list of books.

Deep Work by Cal Newport
Flow: The Psychology of Optimal Experience by
Mihaly Csikszentmihalyi
The Practicing Mind by Thomas M. Sterner
Willpower by Roy F. Baumeister
Grit by Angela Duckworth
The One Thing by Gary Keller
Essentialism by Greg McKeown
Mastery by Robert Greene
Letters from a Stoic by Seneca
The Art of Living by Epictetus
The Obstacle is the Way by Ryan Holiday
Meditations by Marcus Aurelius

The Daily Stoic by Ryan Holiday
Man Up by Bedros Keuilian
The Little Black Book of Workout Motivation by
Mike Matthews
The Perfect Day Formula by Craig Ballantyne

## ABOUT THE AUTHOR

I'm Chad Howse, the author of this book which has become a labor of love of sorts, a passion project that has seen many different formats and edits and reformations.

As I wrote in the preface, this is as much an exercise in understanding discipline than it is a lesson in discipline. What didn't work, didn't make it into the pages of the book. What helped me, and continues to help me to this day, did.

I am not the world's most disciplined human. When you think of that fella you think of a perpetual early riser who doesn't touch the drink nor the smoke. While I perpetually rise early, about once a week I'll smoke a cigar, and a couple times a week - at least

- I'll enjoy some wine or scotch or beer. While I train religiously every second day, I don't follow a restrictive diet, in fact, I actually follow *my own diet*, The Man Diet (www.themandietbook.com).

I'm a work in progress. To use that word again, a perpetual work in progress.

While I'm constantly trying to find clarity on where I'm going and what I'm doing, I've at least realized that the habits must be consistent, the effort must be constant and persistent, to take it easy is to regress as a human. No matter the lack of clarity in the moment, I've realized that the effort must be a constant because of this idea that the man worthy of success gains it, and the man who is not worthy of it doesn't.

If you take anything from the book, please read the section on Ben Franklin over again. He identified who this man was, how he lived and acted, and became him as quickly as he could, and lo and behold, the success he craved came, and compounded.

You have that in you, that potential, that capacity to deserve what you want, you just have to bridge that gap between who you are and who you need to become every single fucking day.

Life ain't easy, nor should we expect it to be. We should expect tribulation and revel in facing it erect, like a man.

Now, about me personally, I live in Calgary, Alberta, a beautiful town with even more beautiful neighboring mountains, the Canadian Rockies. I have a lovely little dog, a 110 pound dogo Argentino, named Teddy. An absolutely wonderful lady. I'm new to hiking, hunting, shooting, archery, and fishing, and I'm new to them simply because I was raised to be an athlete, to compete, to play hockey and then basketball and then fight in the ring, the outdoors wasn't a focus growing up, but as you move beyond the sports - being not good enough to go pro in any of them - you search for new challenges and adventures and the lot of activities above have provided that.

And about how and who I was raised by, I'm lucky.

Most of the lessons in this book were taught to me by both my Mom and my Dad, even my Nonna, Nana, and Poppa. I lucked out beyond belief by being born to those parents. That pure fortune hasn't gone unnoticed, and the fact that being such a beneficiary as to be born to wise, intelligent, hard-working, honorable, and *good* people, I can't waste that gift living in a half-assed manner.

What's your gift?

In the book I mention how Jerry Seinfeld saw Richard Prior's seemingly horrible upbringing as advantage when it came to comedy. And the slough of silver-spoon fed humans who do nothing with the advantages they've been given is apparent by the lack of generational wealth in America. So it's all perspective.

This book is the second book I've written, and a third is being worked on as soon as this one's complete. Hopefully this in some way helped you as much as it did me, and if there's anything at all I can help with, and you *don't* want to get the audiobook for free at thelostartofdiscipline.com/audio - where you'll get my email - then head here where you'll get a free program, as well as my personal email, and I'd really appreciate hearing from you: https://daremightythings.lpages.co/10days/

For FREE Bonus Materials Head to thelostartofdiscipline.com/resources

For your FREE audiobook head to: thelostartofdiscipline.com/audio

Printed in Great Britain
by Amazon